Big Pharma
Big Agri
Big Conspiracy

A New World Order Spin on Drugs and GMOs

By Dina Rae

June 28, 2014

DRPublications

Introduction

Big Pharma's and Big-Agri's growing power happens mostly behind the scenes. For whatever reason, mainstream media leaves these giants alone except in terms of business profit margins. Before researching the two industries, I knew nothing more than most people-a vague recognition of the terms Big Pharma and Big Agri. A few magazines articles along with some radio talk show episodes was all it took to ensnare me into obsession.

As curiosity turned into research, I could not help but speculate that these industries are involved in conspiracy on a global level. This is a subject that impacts anyone who has ever taken medication, seen a doctor, and/or eaten food. If you are intrigued about the elite inner circle of these two empires, *Big Pharma, Big Agri, and Big Conspiracy* is the perfect place to begin your journey in searching for the proverbial man behind the curtain. This book is an introduction to history, fact, and conspiracy theory of these growing industries. A follow-up book is currently being outlined. For the record, I am NOT a doctor, just a nerd who loves to learn new things.

About the author:

Author Dina Rae has four published novels in thriller, horror, and paranormal genres. Her passion for conspiracy theory is obvious as she continues to mix fact into her fiction, leaving readers wondering about the truth. She holds a Master of Arts from Roosevelt University. Ms. Rae continues to guest on multiple conspiracy radio shows, convinced that New World Order looms around the corner. *Big Agri, Big Pharma, and Big Conspiracy* is her first nonfiction book.

What is Big Pharma?

Big Pharma is a term that refers to the giants of the pharmaceutical industry. Collectively, they made approximately $690 billion in 2012 and are projected to exceed one trillion in 2014. That's more than the GDP of Saudi Arabia and Iraq combined. Because of the immense profitability, many question the ethics involved in research, FDA approval, manufacturing, and prescriptions of the pharmaceuticals. Big Pharma doesn't just sell pharmaceuticals; they influence the entire healthcare industry.

Who is Big Pharma?

Generally, Big Pharma consists of the biggest drug companies who make more than three billion dollars each year. Of the top eleven giants, six are headquartered in the U.S. These companies spend multi-millions of dollars each year to lobby Congress for legislation in their favor. U.S. pharmaceutical companies reportedly have 1,100 lobbyists who make sure they are represented.

Whose political campaigns are funded by Big Pharma?

In 2012 Big Pharma favored the Republicans, but they also hedged their bets by backing the Democrats. About $16.2 million was spent by the top twenty pharmaceutical companies for Democratic and Republican campaign contributions. The top three that donated over one million dollars in campaign funds were Pfizer, Amgen, and Abbott, with Merck a few dollars shy of one million.

Some of the biggest giants are listed below.

(based on 2012 pharmaceutical revenues in billions)

http://www.drugwatch.com/manufacturer/

Manufacturer	*2012 in Billions*
Johnson & Johnson	*$67.2*
Pfizer	*$58.9*
Novartis	*$56.7*
Roche	*$47.8*
Merck	*$47.3*
Sanofi	*$46.4*
GlaxoSmithKline	*$39.9*
Abbot Lab	*$39.9*
Astra Zeneca	*$28*
Bayer	*$24.3*

Johnson & Johnson: They sell drug-store drugs like Tylenol, Band-Aids, and baby shampoo. Ethicon, a subsidiary of Johnson and Johnson, makes surgical items. One of their products, a vaginal mesh implant, is currently under fire. They have 1800 lawsuits filed against them.

Pfizer: Lipitor (cholesterol problems), Viagra (erectile dysfunction), Celebrex (arthritis), and Lyrica (neuropathic pain) are some of their most advertised. Despite their huge sales, they claim huge overhead in taxes, advertising, and research and development. Later on I will go more into R&D, as they really aren't paying for all that is claimed. The tax-payer unwittingly pays for much of their R&D.

Novartis: Gilenya (Multiple Sclerosis) and Diovan (hypertension) are some of their top sellers.

Merck: Singulair for asthma and Zetia for cholesterol are some of their big movers. They also manufacture several vaccines.

Abbott Labs: Klacid (antibiotic), Biaxin (bacterial infections), Luvox (anti-depressant), and Synthroid (thyroid) are some of their many products.

Big Pharma claims they are in the business of curing and controlling diseases. Their real mission, like all businesses, is to increase profits. Unlike most businesses they do not have to play by the same rules. Their twenty-year patents given out for each of their new drugs give them a monopoly. This prevents other countries from making cheaper versions. TRIPS (international intellectual property rights organization) legally protects them from others cutting into their profits.

Can they patent plants found in remote places of the world?

Yes. They can and they do, especially in the rain forest, through a process called bio-prospecting. They get away with it by paying indigenous people a stipend for exploration of new plants. To patent something suggests that it's an invention. How are plants grown in the rain forest an invention? Again, Big Pharma does not have to play by the rules. They pay for the legislation that enables them to take what they want.

Many of these companies will protect their empires at any and all costs. Lying to Federal Drug Administration, submitting fraudulent data, bribing doctors, omitting side effects, and bullying the supplement industry are some of the ways they play ball. Lastly, some conspiracy theories claim Big Pharma hide cures to terrible diseases to continue steady, gigantic profits.

What is Big-Agri?

This book began with exploring the inner workings of Big-Pharma from a lay-person's perspective. My research constantly overlapped another mammoth industry called Big-Agri.

Big-Agri is short for big agriculture or farming corporations that are taking over the farming industry on a global level. This kingdom controls many aspects of farming such as crop production through technology and pesticides. One of their main contributions to the world's food supply is the controversial use of GMOs or genetically modified organisms. Later on in this book I will elaborate on GMOs. GM stands for genetically modified and then there is the term GE for genetically engineered. These terms basically mean the same thing and will be used interchangeably for the purposes of this book. GM/GE/GMOs are a growing business of genetically engineered food.

GMOs have led to other modified things such as glow-in-the dark cats, cabbage with scorpion venom, less flatulent cows, vaccinated bananas, cancer medicine eggs, and mass carbon eating plants. The possibilities are endless, producing results that make for a great horror/sci-fi movie. Much of the GMO food has earned the nickname "Franken-food".

The giant corporations that make up Big-Agri are Dow AgroSciences, DuPont, Monsanto, and Syngenta. Other corporations that make up the business include machinery (John Deere), ADM (grain transport), and AB Agri (animal feeds, micro-ingredients, and biofuels). In this book, I will be referring to Big-Agri in strictly crops, food, or pesticides.

Monsanto (largest seed and pesticide manufacturer in the world)

In 2013 fiscal year Monsanto's net sales were $14,861,000,000. Net profits were $7,653,000,000. That's a gross profit of 51%! They reported a net income of $2,482,000,000 after research and development and other expenses. Research and Development costs will later on be more fully explored. At face value, according to their own site, www.monsanto.com, that's about 17% profits-not a bad return!

DuPont, www.dupont.com

This corporation has its fingers in many pies, including healthcare/Big-Pharma. For the purpose of this book, DuPont will be placed among the Big-Agri companies. Some of their biggest selling products are herbicides/insecticides and GMO seeds. Their agriculture products division had an outstanding 2013-9.9 billion in sales, primarily through their GMO corn seeds. Seven million acres planted their corn in 2013 compared to two million acres using the seeds in 2012.
Dow-AgroSciences,
http://www.dowagro.com/products/

Their main products are herbicides/insecticides and GMO seeds. Dow-AgroSciences is a subsidiary of Dow-Chemical. Their gross sales in 2012 was $6,400,000,000. A little interesting trivia found on their own website shows that Dow AgroSciences was originally called DowElanco and then joined with Dow Chemical and Elanco Plant Sciences. Why is this important? Because Elanco Plant Sciences is part of Eli Lilly, one of the Big-Pharma mammoths earlier mentioned. Big Agri and Big Pharma are constantly overlapping.

Syngenta, www.sygenta.com

This global corporation's main products are herbicides, insecticides, fungicides, and GMO seeds including flowers. In 2012 they grossed 14,202,000,000 in sales with $6,984,000,000 in gross profits. $2,292,000,000 was left over after operating expenses. Syngenta is still a young company.   According to their website, they offered to invest one half of a billion dollars in Africa at the 2012 G8 Summit. Humanitarian or smart business? Syngenta projects that they will sell 25 billion dollars in sales by 2020.

Throughout this book I will present the facts and cite sources. Some sources will be hyperlinked and other sources will be mentioned on the bibliography page of the book. The conspiracy angle is yours to agree or disagree with. At the very least, you will hopefully have a different perspective on this very important subject.

Chapter One: Codex Alimentarius
Chapter Two: FDA and USDA: Puppets or Protectors?
Chapter Three: What is a GMO?
Chapter Four: Most Harmful Chemicals in Food
Chapter Five: Organics
Chapter Six: Natural Remedies
Chapter Seven: The Rise of Anti-Depressants
Chapter Eight: ADD/ADHD: Is it a Real Disorder?
Chapter Nine: Why Are Medical Bills and Drugs so High?
Chapter Ten: Black Box Drugs
Chapter Eleven: Vaccines: Prevention or Profit?
Conclusion/Bibliography

Chapter One

Codex Alimentarius: What is it and why is it important to Big Pharma?

New World Order Conspiracy Theory

In order to understand how the Codex works, it is imperative to understand the concept of New World Order conspiracy theory also known as globalization and one world government. New World Order or NWO universally refers to an elite group of people who belong to the inner circles of government, industry, media, religion, academia, and other influential segments of society. These people actively conspire to abandon all boundaries of nations. Why? Because once the world abolishes all nations and cultures it can then be restructured under one rule.

Yes, it sounds crazy, but the Bible has plenty to say about the subject. In Genesis God scatters everyone to the four corners of the earth after the Tower of Babel story. In this story people began speaking the same language. Some clergy believe this detail signifies a breakdown of different cultures. Therefore, this story documents the world's first attempt at a one world government. In Revelation the Bible ends with the world being ruled by the Anti-Christ who is eventually defeated by Jesus. The United Nations and/or European Union and/or Bilderberg meetings and/or certain global alliances are examples of the onset of New World Order. Jerry Jenkins and Tim LaHaye best lay out a realistic example of this scenario in their best-selling *Left Behind* series.

Whether you are a religious fanatic, tin-foil hat wearing freak, or plain old average Joe, you have to wonder if this theory holds weight. Every now and then the elite lose their control and an insider goes rogue, something doesn't end up destroyed, and mistakes are made, allowing us common folk a glimpse of what could/will be. By the way, NWO spells *own* backwards.

Under NWO, there will be one currency and one set of laws. Those who don't agree and don't comply with the new government will be exterminated.

Most conspiracy theorists believe one of the biggest goals of the New World Order elite is depopulation. This involves exterminating all who are uneducated, poor, physically or mentally impaired, and/or in some way a hindrance to power. The total world population would be shaved down to under one billion people.

The elite inner circles have somewhat of a valid argument for murder. Population in the world has exploded exponentially since the 1800's. If this trend continues, the world won't be big enough to feed or medicate everyone. This is how Big-Pharma and Big-Agri fit into the conspiracy.

Who/what is the inner circle?

Conspiracy theorists believe secret societies such as Freemasons, Illuminati, Council of Foreign Relations, Trilateral Commission, Club of Rome, Bohemian Grove, Skull and Bones, and all who attend the annual Bilderberg meetings are the elite behind globalization. George H. Bush, Joe Biden, and Prime Minister Gordon Brown have used the term in international speeches. Organizations such as United Nations, World

Trade Organization, International Monetary Fund, NATO, G-8, and the European Union seem to align their policies with globalism/globalization.

Agenda 21 is a U.N. directive that outlines "sustainable development", a term that lends fuel for New World Order theory. Some believe this agenda is a passive, sugar-coated way of depriving people of their personal property, keeping the population under constant surveillance, and eventually depopulating the world. Some of the wording also implies that "equality" really means communism.

Diehard fanatics against the agenda include obscure pockets of the media, preppers, End-of-Days Christians, liberal tree-huggers, organic farmers, victims of fatal prescriptions, disgruntled whistle-blowers, and anyone who questions the mainstream media and heads of state. The Internet, local cable TV channels, radio, and small publishers are the most likely to cover related New World Order stories. My novel, *The Last Degree*, fictionalizes this event and how it could play out.

So what does this have to do with food?

Henry Kissinger once said, "If you control the food supply, you control the people." Codex Alimentarius is one of the major puzzle pieces that make this statement true.

Codex Alimentarius technically means food code or food book. It's a volume of food standards/guidelines and trade regulations, claiming that the world would be a better place if there were universal rules applied to food and supplements. They claim they want to harmonize food standards.

The Codex is comprised of one hundred eighty-six members, two hundred and fifteen observers, forty-nine Intergovernmental Regulation Organizations (IGOs), one hundred fifty Nongovernmental Organizations (NGOs), and sixteen U.N. members. The members break off into twenty-seven committees and keep the Codex up to date. Two of these committees, Food Labeling and Nutrient and Foods for Special Uses, are the most important.

Critics of the Codex think the code is a means to annihilate the natural supplements and organic industries. The way the food standards are laid out within the Codex suggests this to be true. For example, genetically modified organisms (GMOs) do not have to be listed on ingredient labels. GMOs will be discussed in more detail in a separate chapter. GMO seeds are used in crops for resistance to pests, weather, and certain herbicides.

No one can guarantee GMO safety to consumer's health. Farming conglomerates like GMOs because they quickly increase their crops with desired traits. Those who are suspicious believe GMOs are to blame for allergies, disorders, and illnesses. They have strong arguments that accuse GMOs of being toxic. Monsanto and DuPont are some of the world's primary GMO producers for agri-business. In Europe, GMOs are given priority to farming. For example, France designated one acre of available farmland for organics and three acres for GMO crops.

History of Codex Alimentarius
A brief history of Codex Alimentarius's onset begins with Nazi Germany. The

pharmaceutical corporation I.G. Farben consisted of multiple drug companies pre-WWII such as Bayer and BASF. It was I.G. Farben's profits that catapulted Hitler to power and I.G. Farben's top board members who controlled several concentration camps. Auschwitz was owned by the company and ran by its directors. I.G. Farben invented the gasses used for extermination of the prisoners. Those who weren't gassed to death, worked for I.G. Farben in some capacity, some serving as lab guinea pigs for heinous experiments with goals of inventing more profitable drugs.

Fritz Ter Meer, I.G. Farben's director, was in charge of the immense work camp. He was responsible directly and indirectly for murdering millions of Auschwitz's prisoners. During the Nuremburg Trials, he was sentenced to seven years, serving less than three. Once released, he continued working for the dismantled I.G. Farben as Bayer's top official. He is believed to be the creator of Codex Alimentarius. The huge bureaucracy behind the Codex always denied Nazi ties, yet has refused to name the chief architects. The Food and Agriculture Organization (FAO) and World Health Organization (WHO) also had a great deal to do with its formation.

Even with Nazis prior involvement, you might be wondering what the Codex has to do with New World Order. This is where it gets confusing, but then it's supposed to be confusing. The average person is supposed to get weary, therefore giving their curiosity a rest. Other organizations were created as a way to make the Codex (the book of harmless food guidelines) a powerful legal means of enforcing part of their New World Order agenda.

What organizations use the Codex for a legal tool?

Without getting too off track, the World Trade Organization (WTO), established in 1995, sets rules about international trade between the world's trading nations. WTO is supposed to protect trade agreements and negotiations, and also settle disputes. For years there has been international talks that sift through every detail of the WTO's powers so that everyone from the one hundred fifty-seven participating countries felt represented.

When disputes arise between trading nations of foods and supplements, the WTO uses the Codex Alimentarius for making rulings on trade. In other words, Business A refuses to follow the "harmonizing" guidelines of the Codex. A complaint is made to the WTO. WTO investigates and then withdraws Business A's trading privileges along with other crippling sanctions. Business A loses mass profits and might even have to dissolve its business. So in the nutshell, the Codex is not "law" but is backed by the WTO in trade dispute decisions, turning it into a set of rules that have economic repercussions. Many nations have to change their laws to fit in with the Codex's standards.

Why is it so hard for businesses to follow international trading rules?

Some of the rules aren't fair-especially to the vitamin, mineral, herb, and natural supplement industry. Despite constant studies that show amazing healing and medicinal properties of natural products, Codex Alimentarius's rules have left this industry out in the cold while allowing Big Pharma to take over the natural arm of health, nutrition, and medicine. For example, most of Europe has very low doses of gingko, vitamin D3, vitamin C, and calcium available to the consumer. This limits all benefits of the supplement. Many natural food vendors worry that common foods such as peppermint and garlic will eventually be classed as drugs, allowing Big Pharma to swoop in to patent and then prescribe.

Dr. Matthias Rath of the Rath Foundation is very vocal about the benefits of vitamins. He has much to say about his own studies on the role of vitamin C. He believes many diseases are caused by vitamin deficiencies, but those hooked up with Big Pharma and the Codex want to suppress this information.

Presently, the U.S. is not part of the Codex but wants to "harmonize" with their standards. The only thing keeping them back is DSHEA (Dietary Supplement Health Education Act of 1994) which is the result of a grassroots movement by the health and nutrition industry in reaction to the

Codex's gaining power jab. The Codex's influence is constantly threatening the status quo.

Chapter Two

FDA and USDA: Puppets or Protectors?

FDA: How do they fit into the conspiracy?

FDA stands for Food and Drug Administration. They are a U.S. agency that regulates food and drugs with the intention of protecting the consumer from harmful products and practices. They are part of the Department of Health and Human Services. The FDA is headquartered in Silver Spring, Maryland, employs eleven thousand people, and costs the American taxpayers about 2.6 billion dollars a year.

The FDA oversees a wide range of big business such as food, beverages, and their labeling, prescription drug approval and labeling, cosmetics, medical devices, veterinary food and drugs, radiation-emitting products, alcohol, and tobacco. Obviously this agency wields a great deal of power. New legislation is constantly expanding their limits. One of the most recent examples would be the 2011 Food Safety Modernization Act which gives the FDA control of the safety of U.S.

food supply and imported products. Time will tell how this new act will be interpreted, abused, and exploited.

The FDA was the brainchild of the Rockefeller family. Hence, its birth was shrouded in conspiracy. But even before the Rockefellers, elements of the FDA can be traced back as far as the 1540s in England. In 1540 Parliament decided that the practice of medicine had to be approved by a college of surgeons. This new law was backed up by one of Rome's most powerful bishops. By 1546 the Herbalist Charter was created to draft rules for healers, and then later adopted by the U.S.

Politicians already had their fingerprints on the medical business world. Standard Oil's John D. Rockefeller just helped it along in terms of power and prestige. Although considered one of the greatest philanthropists of all time, Rockefeller's altruism was countered with self-interest. The Rockefeller Foundation, created in 1904 and originally called the General Education Fund, finagled its way into the New York legislature. The foundation honked the horn of the pharmaceutical business at every opportunity.

U.S. involvement in the food and drug industry can be traced as far back as 1848 when Lewis Caleb Clark of the Patent Office carried out a chemical analysis of agricultural products. By 1879 almost one hundred bills involving regulation of food and drugs wound up in Congress. In 1906 President Roosevelt signed the Food and Drugs Act also known as the Wiley Act. This legislation led to the Bureau of Chemistry, the FDA's original name.

Early FDA's duties rested more upon product labeling than drug approval of pharmaceuticals. They listed the weight/measure of food products and harmful ingredients like alcohol, heroin, and cocaine. The FDA was relatively a benign bureaucracy that set some helpful standards for American consumers.

Problems of food contamination produced public hysteria. Upton Sinclair's The Jungle only added fuel to the public outrage. The Bureau of Chemistry/FDA seemed like the logical place to begin regulation.

Meanwhile, Rockefeller donated millions of dollars to the medical colleges of Harvard, Yale, John Hopkins, and other prestigious campuses of the era. His donations had strings. His most trusted employees sat on the board of directors of these medical schools that accepted his money. Rockefeller's influence in medical academia created a monopoly within the chemical/pharmaceutical industry. Ironically, Rockefeller preferred the holistic approach to health problems over prescriptions and lived until ninety-eight years old.

Rockefeller's medical monopoly is still in place. Traditional doctors prefer prescriptions over prevention, making Big-Pharma a 700 billion dollar business annually. Doctors who practice holistic treatments were and still are deemed as quacks.

Rockefeller saw early on the threat of natural medicine. For example, he encouraged China to change their Eastern philosophy of medicine by paying forty-five million dollars to Peking Union Medical College. Acceptance of his generous donation meant replacing herbal remedies with drugs patented in the U.S, thus westernizing the world in medicine. His vision was backed in several pieces of legislation.

No one can question the good that Rockefeller, AMA, and Big-Pharma have done to advance healthcare. However, their triumphs are often tainted with conspiracies of poisonous products found in drugs or foods that are ignored and then approved by their 'friends' who sit on the board of the FDA. Conspiracies shroud the pharmaceuticals used for cancer, AIDS, Alzheimer's, heart disease, MS, Major Depression, ADD/ADHD, and other diseases/disorders.

FDA began as a simple regulatory agency that turned into a major super power in the drug world. Their approval means everything to Big Pharma's profits. Most believe they take painful precautions to ensure consumers that new drugs are almost perfectly safe. The average consumer believes various pills/food chemicals/cell phones (yes, anything that emits radiation)/cosmetics/GMOs have been in clinical trials, studied and tested for years and years, even decades, before becoming available for public consumption .

Isn't the FDA extremely thorough and particular, often taking a prolonged amount of time for drug approval?

Maybe in the old days, but due to the spread of AIDS in the '80s and '90s legislation has reshaped their role in the approval process. This is the standard way most drugs get approved.

Step 1: Clinical trials are completed, usually a forty-eight week to one year process. Most trials follow-up for months/years afterward before submitting to FDA, and are usually divided into two or three phases.

Step 2: The pharmaceutical company files a New Drug Application (NDA) with FDA's Center for Drug Evaluation and Research (CDER). This consists of volumes of paperwork.

Step 3: If CDER believes there is enough information, the NDA is passed onto an advisory committee made up of non-FDA experts. They can take as long as twelve months before beginning a review, and then another six months to go over the NDA-that's another year and a half. A special committee, Antiviral Drugs Advisory Committee (ADAC), specialize in HIV research and care.

Step 3A: If ADAC gets the NDA, then there is a public meeting for the FDA to hear both the pros and cons of the drug. At the end of the meeting, ADAC members vote on drug approval. If they vote for the anti-viral drug, then the FDA almost always approves it via a letter to the pharmaceutical company within days/weeks of the public meeting. Almost all of the anti-HIV drugs have been approved. The FDA only needs two positive trials to approve the drug.

Does this seem thorough or particular? What about the trials that were negative?

Again, only two positive trials are needed.

What's wrong with the development of new drugs?

Before the mid-1980's this system worked pretty well. Big Pharma grew rich while new life-saving/life-changing drugs were invented. Everyone was happy, right?

The creation and testing of new drugs prior to the mid-1980's went something like this: a pharmaceutical company gave a medical school/university their drug to test with no strings attached. They were not allowed to get involved in the design of the test, analysis, or publication of the results.

The beginning of this obscene greed begins with the Bayr-Dole Act (1980). This act essentially opened the doors for publically funded universities and medical schools to patent their own discoveries and license their patent to one of the Big Pharma companies for royalties. Big Pharma showers them with money. Therefore, medical schools and universities are now essentially their business partners. Some people would go as far as saying that schools and universities are Big Pharma's employees.

Since Bayr-Dole, drug companies do less and less of the basic research in new drugs. They have their "business partners"/medical schools do the ground work. Because medical schools are being paid through royalties, they are now biased to test results. Some people argue that Big Pharma is basically paying for test results. Big Pharma has not surprisingly got more involved with the way their new drug is tested. Universities need special permission to publish the results of their findings. In some instances, they aren't allowed to see the results. The FDA does see the results, at least by law they are supposed to see all of the results. They don't release the negative results and only need two positive results to approve a drug.

True/False: The FDA is too cautious with new drug approval and takes much too long.

Depends. Back in the old days this would have been one hundred-percent true, but not anymore. The fact is that the FDA is faster than other regulatory agencies. Per 1992 PDUFA (Prescription Drug User Fee Act) they are paid a user fee by the drug company for the sole purpose of speeding up the process. The user fees cover half of the FDA's overhead. Over the years PDUFA has also sped up the approval process for medical devices.

What happens after approval?

Step 4: While the FDA is reviewing the NDA/new drug application and volumes of paper are filed, the pharmaceutical company is producing mass quantities of their new drug because they expect approval. With the HIV drugs, this usually pays off. The drug is available within days of the FDA's formal approval.

What is Expanded Access?

It's fast-track FDA approval of drugs before clinical trials are finished. Again, this loophole requires a lot of paperwork and was created due to the AIDs epidemic. A new approach to a rush on approval is called the parallel track, again created because of AIDs. These usually take place in a national study that any doctor who treats HIV-positive patients can participate in. These fast-track programs still require a ton of paperwork that doctors don't have time for. AIDs patients with private insurance seemed to have better luck in getting their doctors to participate.

Approval for herbs and vitamins is a little different. FDA does not consider them drugs (at this point). They are handled by the Center for Food Safety and Applied Nutrition (CFSAN). This group uses guidelines for safety described in 1994

DSHEA (a law that so far has protected the supplemental industry from lengthy approval and scrutiny). The FDA can only ban dietary supplements when doctors and/or consumers file reports that state the supplement in question is unsafe and/or the supplement is claiming that it has medicinal properties.

Sounds Like a Good System, Right?

It's certainly an expensive system. On average it costs Big Pharma one billion dollars to go through the process. They have "ensured" their new drug approval by stacking the deck with yes-men. Since 2008 seventy-five people have been charged with supplying inside information on patents and mergers that center around new drug approvals. For example, FDA chemist Cheng Yi Liang plead guilty to insider trading on twenty-five companies.

Besides the 'bad apples' within the agency, there are other kinks in the chain. A few decades ago the procedure for FDA approval tipped the balance of power toward on the FDA's side. For instance, before FDA approval the drug's trial results are published in a highly respected medical journal by a doctor. In today's world many doctors no longer write the articles about drug trials. Ghostwriters hired by the drug companies are the real authors. The drug companies provide them with the information about their new drug. That's kind of like an author writing his/her own book review. It's of course going to be five stars and a masterpiece. Again, when the FDA looks at the trials they see many of the negative results, but only need two positive results. The negative results are not published.

Patent Controversy

A patent on anything is a legal protection that prevents copycats from stealing others' ideas. In theory, it gives inventors incentive for discovery, knowing that they will be the sole beneficiary of potential profits. In the pharmaceutical world it means a monopoly on profit. The patent usually takes effect while the drug is being tested (not approved). The typical patent length is twenty years, but once all of the testing and research is finished, there could be as little as eight years left on the patent once it's ready for the market place. In theory, once the patent expires, then generic versions of the drug hit the market, causing the cost to go way down.

However, there is a legal way to extend the monopoly. Another patent can be filed for an "improved" version of the drug. These are called "Me Too" drugs. Some of the well-known examples are Lipitor's transformation into Crestor and Prilosec (now over-the-counter drug) evolving into Nexium. Big Pharma claims that the patents are a necessary evil of the business because for every drug that makes it into the market, there are four drugs that never make it into the laboratory. Research is very expensive.

Family USA, a healthcare advocate group, discredits this argument.

Among the nine pharmaceutical companies examined in the report... all but one spent more than twice as much on marketing, advertising, and administration than they did on research and development... Six out of the nine companies made more money in net profits than they spent on research and development last year.

According to Family USA, it is the advertising and executive salaries that make pharmaceuticals so expensive, at least in the U.S. Everywhere else the product is substantially cheaper. Federal research grants and funds raised by charities provide plenty of money for research as well. And then there are the taxpayers-you and me. We all pay for the "expensive" research that is used as an excuse for high prices. It's corporate welfare. The welfare that the poor receive makes up about 3% of the federal budget. Corporate welfare makes up 17% of the federal budget. The American people pay twice-first for funding in research to prove drug is safe, and then at the pharmacy after doctor prescribes the drug.

What happens when the patent wears out?

Big Pharma makes a new and improved drug that is tested against a placebo (sugar pill) instead of being tested against the old drug with the expired patent. Plus, the new drug only has to be slightly different. All the chemist has to do is change a molecule and poof-a "new" drug. A smart marketing campaign that targets the users of the drug manipulates them into thinking the drug that they are on is out dated and they need to switch over to the "better" one even though it is more expensive. Again, many people don't pay for their drugs. Their insurance pays.

There is also the exclusivity concept that gives the pharmaceutical company exclusive rights on marketing the drug. Here's the kicker-the right of exclusivity does not have to coincide with the length of the patent, despite the fact that both of these legal tools do the same thing-continue the monopoly on the drug.

Does Big Pharma have a monopoly on an international level?

Technically no, but actually yes. TRIPS or international intellectual property rights protects the intellectual work of authors, composers, singers, artists, and even patents-specifically pharmaceutical patents. In other words, a drug patented in the U.S. cannot be copied and sold in New Zealand. This means that the same 20-year U.S. patent applies all over the world-even for life-saving drugs. Other countries are always trying to bend the law, and at times proven to be successful.

One of the main reasons attached to saving the rainforest is the exotic plants that are in danger of extinction. Many doctors and researchers hope to find the next blockbuster drug (a drug that has at least one billion dollars in sales) in the jungle. Miracle plants have been found in the past. For example, Quinine, the first anti-malarial medicine, is made from bark in South America.

Bio-prospecting or hunting for natural remedies in lands that one does not own is part of Big Pharma's business model. If Big Pharma tries to steal the plant without compensating the natives from the plant's natural habitat, then it's called bio-piracy. In the 1990s the University of Mississippi Medical Center was granted a U.S. patent for turmeric. Turmeric is a spice in chicken curry. Indians not only cook with it, but also use it to heal wounds and cure diseases. Because of TRIPS (the international intellectual property law), the U.S. patent made it illegal to use the spice for medicinal purposes. After two years of global complaining from both the U.S. and India (where it comes from), the World Trade Organization declared the spice unable to be patented. Turmeric has been used for medical purposes for over 2000 years. Despite India's legal win, companies are still hot for a turmeric patent and will probably try again to patent the spice.

Who gets appointed to the FDA? Puppets or professionals?

The FDA has often been criticized for being a revolving door for lawyers and businessmen who have ties to Big-Pharma and Big Agri. Many scream conflict of interest. Posts are appointed. The FDA's organization consists of the Office of the Commissioner and four directorates who oversee the agency's core functions. The FDA's website shows Dr. Margaret A. Hamburg as the Commissioner. Dr. Hamburg's resume/bio is listed on the FDA site. Some of the more interesting accomplishments include a Harvard degree and extensive research on neuroscience at Rockefeller University. She later focused on AIDs research at the National Institute of Allergy and

Infectious Diseases. She was also involved in the Nuclear Threat Initiative, a foundation dedicated to reducing the threat of nuclear, bio and chemical weapons. One of her major initiatives is Globalization which many believe is a crucial step needed in creating New World Order. Her words suggest that the FDA should have international responsibilities.

"Global production of FDA-regulated products has quadrupled over the last decade and continues to grow. Today, FDA-regulated products originate from more than 150 countries, 130,000 importers and 300,000 foreign facilities. Fifty percent of fresh fruits, 20 percent of vegetables, and 80 percent of seafood consumed in America comes from abroad. Similarly, 40 percent of finished drugs come from overseas, and 80 percent of active ingredients manufacturers are located outside the US. Further, half of all medical devices are imported. The growth in imports has been rapid and promises to accelerate.

Globalization has fundamentally altered the economic and security landscape and demands a

major change in the way FDA fulfills its mission.
Over the next decade, FDA will transform from a
predominantly domestically-focused agency
operating in a globalized economy to a modern
public health regulatory agency fully prepared for a
complex globalized regulatory environment.

The agency is already working to increase
transparency and accountability in the supply
chain, developing better enforcement and
regulatory tools, encouraging greater responsibility
by industry, and enhancing collaboration with
international regulatory counterparts and other
third parties.

As our world transforms and becomes
increasingly globalized, it is vital that we come
together as a global community – in new,
unprecedented, and even unexpected ways – to
build a public health safety net for consumers
around the world."

This initiative was cut and pasted from
FDA.gov. Notice the underlined parts. They mirror
the Codex Alimentarius ideology and New World
Order conspiracy theory.

Here are some other top bureaucrats who run the FDA. Please note their gleaned biographies.

Michael Taylor, Deputy Commissioner for Foods and Veterinary Medicine as of 2009, is perhaps the most controversial of the FDA appointments. His post did not exist until President Obama. His biography on the FDA.org website conveniently skips a large part of his resume. He is important enough to get a Wikipedia page. He worked for King and Spalding, a law firm linked to Monsanto. He has published papers that align with Monsanto products in terms of safe levels of toxicity/carcinogens. Many critics in the organic food industry disagree with Taylor's findings. In 1991 he worked in a different position at the FDA and signed a Federal Register notice that allowed BGH, a steroid given to cows, to be exempt from milk labels.

In 1992 Taylor is thought to have coauthored FDA policy on GMO plant food as a response to growing concern on the safety of

GMOs. Many scientists feared that GMOs were linked to diseases and allergens. This policy protected the use of GMOs by treating them as food additives instead of food. This made them subject to food additive legislation which has different standards. Critics believed the legislation was specifically meant to benefit Monsanto without any regard for public safety.

GMOs will be further explored later on in the book. This 1992 policy is very important because it sets up Big-Agri. The policy treats GMOs in food as food additives. Therefore, GMOs are subject to the food additive regulation which has very different standards.

A few years later an activist, Jeremy Rifkin, made trouble for Taylor, accusing him of having a conflict of interest in the FDA approval of rBST. Taylor recused himself during the late stages of approval. Eventually, Taylor moved over to work for the United States Department of Agriculture (USDA) and then returned to King and Spalding. In 2000 he worked for Monsanto as Vice President of Public Policy. Taylor has also worked as an academic, publishing two papers on U.S. aid for

Africa. By the way, the studies were funded by the
Rockefeller Foundation mentioned earlier.
Skeptics blast Taylor as being a lobbyist for
Monsanto and not a bureaucrat who is supposed
to serve the American people.

Stephen P. Spielburg, M.D., Deputy
Commissioner for Medical Products and Tobacco,
has had a long career as a bureaucrat, academic,
and director of two Big Pharma companies, Merck
and Johnson & Johnson. One of his many
accomplishments includes serving as the
Rapporteur for the Pediatric ICH Initiative (ICH E
11) which harmonized pediatric drug development
regulations in Europe, Japan, and the U.S.
Sounds like more globalism? He serves on the
editorial boards of several pediatric and
pharmacology journals.

What is the USDA?
The U.S.D.A. stands for United States
Department of Agriculture. Like the F.D.A., they
have many duties including food safety. This
department goes more into the farming aspect of

food. Like the F.D.A., they have ideas of internationally expanding their regulations.

The U.S.D.A. originated from the Patent Office in 1839. Like today, the Secretary of this office was interested in collecting and distributing different kinds of seeds. Under Lincoln the office became the Department of Agriculture. During the Great Depression the U.S.D.A. and other agencies popped up to provide nutritional information and food handouts to the nation's most poor. Their role expanded throughout the decades.

Today the U.S.D.A. helps farmers and food producers sell their food in the U.S. and foreign countries. They are also involved in overseas aid programs such as USAID, World Food Program, and World Cocoa Foundation.

The U.S.D.A. has been under fire for many things. For the purposes of this book, its close connections with Big-Agri will be the only focus. Like the F.D.A., the U.S.D.A. is stacked with people who appear to be lobbyists. Never say never, but so far the U.S.D.A. has yet to deny any of Monsanto's applications for new GMO crops.

So who are approving their every request? It starts right at the top.

Tom Vilsack, Secretary of Agriculture, was given this post by Obama in 2009. He was Governor of Iowa. His actions for giant farming corporations and GMOs suggest that he favors Big-Agri. In 2005 he blocked local communities from regulating where GMOs were grown. Vilsack also founded and chaired the Governor's Biotechnology Industry Organization, a lobbying group. He has been given the Governor of the Year Award by biotech corporations.

Currently, Vilsack has approved a new two year pilot project that allows GMO companies to environmentally assess their own crops or outsource the job to their preferred analysts. So in other words, Monsanto and DuPont (and others) can run their own tests to see if their products are safe. Kind of like grading your own test back in high school.

Other Big-Agri/Big-Pharma positions that keep business booming are:

President Obama: He is perhaps the biggest GMO lobbyist, but certainly not the only president to toe the Big-Agri line. He is the biggest disappointment to the organic and natural supplement industry. During the 2008 campaign he made several promises that turned out to be the complete opposite of his presidential actions.

The most controversial legislation is the Monsanto Protection Act of 2013. This act received virtually no coverage on mainstream media news channels. However, one cannot argue with the content of HR 933, the Agricultural Appropriations Bill on March 26, 2013. The meat of this bill prevents a governmental shutdown by providing certain agencies such as the USDA and FDA plenty of funding to keep on functioning. The interesting part of this bill is Section 735 also known as the "Monsanto Act" which leaves courts helpless in banning the sale and planting of GMOs even if proven a health risk. In summary, because of this provision, if one can prove that GMOs are dangerous then too bad. There is no legal recourse. This section is known as a "backroom" deal. A petition signed by 250,000 U.S. citizens was ignored when Obama signed it. It expired last September.

By the way, two of Obama's biggest supporters, Bill Gates and George Soros, also have 900,000 shares and 500,000 shares of Monsanto.

Roy Blunt (R-Senator from Missouri which is also Monsanto's HQs)-He helped draft Section 735 for Monsanto. This senator received a quarter million dollars in 2010 from biotech corporations. He is known for earmarks and pork. *Why do the good folks of Missouri keep re-electing him?* This sounds like another conspiracy for another time.

Islam Sidiqui: This man was a former registered lobbyist for Crop Life America, representing the mother lode (BASF, Bayer, Crop Science, Dow, DuPont, FMC, Monsanto, Sumitomo, and Syngenta). His "expertise" led him to governmental positions such as Chief Agricultural Negotiator (appointed by Obama). His negotiating could lead to exponential sales of GMO crops worldwide. He recently resigned from this position. Rumors circulate that he is in line for a cabinet position. He has spent years promoting the safety of GMO foods and stopping labeling legislation. Sidiqui has been quoted as saying that banning GMOs is "denying food to starving people."

Hillary Clinton: This former Secretary of State/potential 2016 Democratic candidate used to work for Rose Law Firm, a firm that held Monsanto as a client.

Donald Rumsfeld: This former Secretary of Defense was also a former board member of Monsanto's Searle Pharmaceuticals. He's connected with several spin-off conspiracies that stem from his former employers' corporations.

Roger Beachy-PhD in Biology: He is the founding president of the Donald Danforth Plant Science Center (part of Monsanto). This man has held a multitude of upstanding academic positions. His research, with Monsanto's help, led him to discovering the world's first genetically modified food crop. It was a tomato that was modified to be resistant to viral infection. This experiment was quickly applied to other vegetables. Since then his career with GMOs has spread all over the realm of Big Agri. He was a director at Monsanto and then, under Obama, became the first director of National Institute of Food and Agriculture (NIFA) and Chief Scientist of USDA. He currently is the director of the New World Food Center. Yes, the New World Food Center. *Could that name pay homage to New World Order?* Food for thought.

Lidia Watrub-Under Bush, Clinton, and Obama she has served under the USDA and EPA. She was also a new technologies coordinator at Monsanto.

Chapter Three

What is a GMO?

GMO is an acronym for genetically modified organism. In other words, it's a process of altering the genetic makeup of various species (usually plants) in order to manipulate crops. This is usually done by inserting one or more genes into a seed so that the plant could grow in cold climates or grow bigger or resist insects or grow faster, etc. There are lots of reasons for doing this. The main reason claims that genetically altering seeds is a way of maximizing crops in order to keep up with the exponential population growth of the world and rising demand for food. Farmers need to grow crops in any available land despite climate differences around the globe. GMO supporters claim that modified crops are necessary for our survival.

GMOs are a very controversial topic. Like Big Pharma, GMO corporations have to go through our old friends the FDA and the USDA to get approval before planting their product. Only a few companies produce GMO seeds. The profit margin is gigantic, like no other business, except the pharmaceutical business. These two giants are not related (yet), but many doctors believe the reason we get sick is related to food. There is no proof that GMO corporations also known as Big Agri are in cahoots with Big Pharma. However, it is not much of a stretch to theorize that the food we eat makes us sick, therefore we go to the doctor who prescribes us medicine-and round and round it goes.

As mentioned before, GMOs are a result of a gene (s) taken from one species and put inside of the DNA of another species to add a desired trait. There is a gene that creates a pesticide when injected into the DNA of corn. This creation keeps the bugs off of the plant, but it can also turn on or off other genes that are not related to the modification. In other words, the plant is altered in more ways than it was supposed to be altered.

Is this gene harmful? Many doctors believe that these "alterations" are responsible for allergies, toxins, nutrient problems, and other health-related issues.

FDA's scientists have questions about poisons, toxins, etc. that are also created when modifying a plant. Many propose that every item modified should be extensively tested. Makes sense, right? One tiny little problem-Monsanto, one of the biggest companies that modifies seeds, has "contributed" to both Houses of Senate and Representatives. One of Monsanto's attorneys was also in charge of FDA policy. As a result of being "in the know", there are no required safety studies. Everyone who eats food is Big-Agri's guinea pig.

To be fair, GMOs are not blindly being whipped up and planted without any testing. Rats were used for GMO soy, corn, and canola. In rat experiments it was found that the nuclei of the cell was misshapen. When using canola GMOs the rats' livers were heavier than before ingesting the canola. When given GMO corn their kidneys and livers were damaged as well as their blood cells changed.

In a 2012 controversial study, Researcher Gilles-Eric Seralini fed Round-up-ready Monsanto corn to ten rats. The rats developed tumors and some of the rats died. The study was published in the Food and Chemical Toxicology Journal and then suspiciously retracted because of pro-GMO criticism of using only ten rats and also for using rats in itself. *Are rats an ineffective animal to experiment with?* Despite Seralini's "bogus" experiment and "bogus" findings, small groups of rats have been used in studies before. In fact, Monsanto did a similar study years earlier with the same number of rats and did not face any criticism at all. Their experiment suggested that their corn was safe.

Who Profits the Most?

Most GMOs are manufactured and sold through Monsanto, Syngenta, Bayer, Dow, and DuPont. Monsanto is the biggest GM (Genetically Modified) manufacturer in the world with over six hundred patents. They invest $2 million a day on research and development. Their patents include their own modifications along with unmodified life forms. Life forms cannot be patented. Take Aloe vera for instance-it's used for healing cuts. One cannot patent this. However, this rule is bent for

Monsanto. Ninety percent of all GMO patents belong to Monsanto and they are Round-up ready. Round-up ready plants are plants that are genetically modified to be resistant to Round-up or glyphosate. In other words, plants that are Round-up ready can have herbicide dumped on them without dying.

Monsanto has been in business since 1901. Originally founded by Coca Cola's John Francis Queeny, Monsanto began its humble origins selling vanilla/vanillin and caffeine. During World War II, Queeney couldn't import chemicals from Europe. He soon created his own chemical products. In 1929 Monsanto became a public corporation and the largest producer of polychlorinated biphenyls (PCBs), a chemical banned in the 1970s.

PCBs are used as lubricants, cutting oils, and hydraulic fluids. They are linked with cancer, immune disorders, birth defects, and death. Monsanto's first PCB plant was built in Sauget, Illinois and Anniston, Alabama in 1935. They soon licensed other manufacturers to make the chemical. Companies such as GE and

Westinghouse used the product. At the same time of its operation, rates of immature birth and fatal death spiked to highest levels. Liver damage, black acne, and other health problems were being reported. PCB was the common denominator. By the 1940s everyone in the chemical industry including Monsanto knew how dangerous PCBs were yet did nothing and even covered it up. PCB damage spread to many others as companies dumped PCBs in lakes and rivers, in particular the Fox Lake River in the Green Bay area. By 1979 after much investigation PCBs are banned.

In Anniston, Alabama, a reported $700 million dollar settlement package was awarded to 20,000 plaintiffs because of PCB pollution allegedly caused by Monsanto and then Solutia, a spin-off company. On a side note, part of the settlement allowed Pfizer (Big-Pharma company) to come in and set up a clinic/research facility that would provide free medicine and screenings.

Monsanto expanded by adding detergent, soap, and plastic production to their business. They were involved in the Manhattan Project.

Post World War II Monsanto settled into the chemical, pesticide, and herbicide business. Anything or anyone who had something to do with agriculture was their primary customer. They were the creators of the infamous Agent Orange used during Vietnam. Agent Orange contaminated several million Vietnamese and killed or disabled 400,000, giving another half of million children birth defects later on. Now that's a weapon of mass destruction.

Decades later, Monsanto paid out $180 million to injured soldiers and families of dead soldiers for the consequences of Agent Orange. Even today, Monsanto is still paying for their chemical mistakes. In Nitro, West Virginia, they built a chemical plant that produced the harmful herbicide found in Agent Orange. The class action suit claims that dioxins from the plant were spread all over the town, ultimately affecting everyone born after 1949.

In 1968, Queeney died without an heir. Edward Block, an engineer at Monsanto, became its president. In 1972 another one of their chemicals, DDT, gets banned for being a health threat. It was sprayed throughout towns for decades to combat Dutch Elm Disease. Scientific studies linked DDT to neurological diseases and cancer. Biologist Rachel Carlson wrote *Silent Spring*, a famous book about the adverse effects of DDT. The book prompted human awareness about its danger.

About one year after the DDT ban, Monsanto developed glyphosate molecule for killing weeds and roots which were falsely marketed as safe. We know this product as Round-Up, one of Monsanto's top worldwide sellers.

In 1985 Monsanto bought Searle Company, a company that produces aspartame. This sweetener is found in sugar-free products such as soda, pudding, ice cream, creamers, juices, and anything that can replace sugar. Aspartame is worth a chapter in its own right.

In the mid to late 1980s, Monsanto's new empire begun peddling GMOs also called GM (genetically modified) through agriculture. By 1994 they came up with the first biotech product called rBGH and rBST-hormones injected into livestock. This is still controversial.

Monsanto then introduced GM/GMO canola oil. An EPA report from the 1990s stated that Monsanto was 5th among US corporations in releasing toxic chemicals to the environment- estimated 37 million pounds worth.

The company concentrated on GM seeds to combat world hunger. Cynics believed this move was primarily meant to increase profits. Remember the glyphosate (Round-Up) mentioned earlier in the chapter? Again, Monsanto came up with GM/GMO crop that would resist the Round-Up which meant that farmers could spray Round-Up weed killer on the plants during growing season and they wouldn't die. Sound potentially dangerous to your health? It's linked with tissue damage, vomiting, and pulmonary problems. Round-up is now found in human urine.

Round-up catapulted Monsanto to the top of agricultural products, along with introducing to our diets more GMO canola, GMO cotton, and GMO corn.

Round-up claimed to be "biodegradable", but this claim could not be substantiated. Due to outside pressure, "biodegradable" had to be removed from the label. Dr. Belle from France claims that Round-up affects cell division and even provokes cancer (The World According To Monsanto).

In the late '90s and early 2000s Monsanto spent billions of dollars across the globe in seed companies. Sound like a monopoly? Monsanto worked out a deal with DuPont to share information about GMOs. Today Monsanto owns 90% of all GMO crops in the world. With the sales of Round-Up, Monsanto is the fifth largest agrochemical company in the world. They expanded their line of GMOs and now have GMO-ready wheat available for farmers.

Besides the health risks that GMOs may pose, there are other problems with this agricultural takeover. GMO seeds are more expensive than traditional seeds which lessens even more profits for the small, private farmer. The GMO seeds have also been inadvertently creating 'super' weeds and 'super' bugs that have adapted to the Round-up ready seeds.

Monsanto kept the government off its back by showering their campaign funds with money. In return they stacked the FDA with their people to make sure new products were approved. As mentioned earlier, Michael Taylor was put on the top rung of the FDA bureaucracy by Obama. Taylor was VP at Monsanto. Conflict of interest? Monsanto's products were and still are criticized for getting FDA approval without any kind of real testing.

The bottom line is this-Monsanto seeds at least 40% of all the U.S. (90% corn and 90% soy) and at least 27% of all the globe. Corn and soy are also used to feed livestock used for meat, eggs, and milk. GMO numbers are growing as Monsanto cuts more and more deals while adding more and more influence in U.S. and international policies.

Companies love their patents, especially the patents that have taken over soy and corn crops. This legal mumbo jumbo is how they manage to monopolize the food industry all over the world.

Before GMO's coup d'état on the agricultural industry, a farmer typically saved his seeds each year to replant. This practice is no longer allowed because of patents on the seeds. Through science and technology, Monsanto, DuPont, and Syngenta have figured out a legal way to monopolize the farming industry. Remember the robber barons? Once Rockefeller, Vanderbilt, Chase, Carnegie, and other giants got too big, the government came in like trust-busting superheroes. But this can't happen in today's world. The patents brilliantly protect today's robber barons not just nationally, but internationally. Farmers have to purchase new seeds each year.

What about the farmers who keep seeds on the sly and hope to replant without getting caught?

Big-Agri has a solution for "cheaters". A Terminator Technology plant was invented for the purpose of germinating one time only so there is no point to keeping the seeds.

What about cross-pollination of the Terminator Technology?

These on-time only seeds caused other plants in nearby farms to become sterile because of the terminator tech trait.

Farmers have to pay a fee based on the size of their crop. Per the GM (genetically modified) agreement, farmers who purchase the GM seeds are not allowed to sue Monsanto. Monsanto's private police force can go onto their property at any time during the first three years of the contract.

What happens when the seeds fail? Can the farmers sue Monsanto for faulty seeds?

No. The seeds are nonrefundable. One of the saddest effects of the GMO seeds is the growing suicide of Indian farmers. Many farmers purchased seeds from Monsanto that never germinated. The farmers were not refunded and charged again for the next year of seeds. Through some kind of financing "deal", the Indian farmers bought more seeds on credit. Their rising debt led to several bankruptcies. Suicide seemed like the only way to absolve other family members from debt.

What about the farmers who don't want GM (Genetically Modified) seeds?

This is the real kicker-when GMO plants get caught up in cross-pollination and end up growing on another farm, the farmer who doesn't use the GM seeds is now in trouble for "stealing" the seeds which are protected under the patent. The farmer has to prove that he/she is not growing GM seeds.

Monsanto encourages other farmers to rat out the farmers who have non-GM crops that are sprinkled with GM plants. Sometimes for as little as a free jacket, farmers will report their neighbors to Monsanto, playing farmers against each other. The next step is the lawsuit. Because of patent law, Monsanto wins. Samples taken from the "thief's" farm are used as "evidence." However, the police are not collecting the samples. Unbelievably, Monsanto pays their own people to collect these samples. Forgive the pun, but could Monsanto *plant* evidence to make a farmer look guilty? Of course they could, but the burden of proof is not on them. Again, it's on the farmer or the proverbial little guy. How is this admissible in court? Logically speaking, I could not find one plausible explanation as to this one-sided system.

Cross-pollination cannot be used as a legal defense for the farmer. It doesn't even matter how much the crop is contaminated-it could be as low as ½ %. Many farmers have reported several kinds of harassment from Monsanto, including thug-like tactics that include using influence with local banks to close farmers' accounts.

The farmers are not the only ones who are "stealing" the GM seeds. Besides cross-pollination, distributing grain has made it almost impossible to separate GMO grain from the organic grain. Soon all crops will be GM crops. Some safeguards have been set up, such as a fifty meter buffer strip in between GM crops and non-GM crops, but it's not enough.

Are GMO food products safe?
The answer to that question depends on who you ask. Monsanto and the U.S. government

say they are safe. They passed all tests that prove that they are no danger to the American people. To use the correct vernacular, GMOs are GRAS which stands for *generally recognized as safe*.

Proponents of organic food, doctors, scientists, academics, and farmers claim that it is not safe. At the very least, GMOs are not as nutritious as organically grown foods. And at the very least, disease such as osteoporosis is linked to a boron deficiency. Cancer rate goes up when there is a selenium deficiency. There have been more studies that suggest other links, making GMOs a controversial topic. Connect the dots and one can see why those who are against GMOs blame GMOs for disease.

What about cows, chicken, and pigs that eat the GMO food?

The food chain taught in high school biology class hasn't changed. What animals eat, we eat. Cows, chickens, and pigs retain most of the pesticides that they eat. Chickens are fed GMO corn along with other chemicals to increase

67

their weight. Besides the GMO corn, chickens are pumped up with hormones, arsenic, antibiotics, and carcinogens. The antibiotics are given because of infections and disease. Chickens are usually kept in very cramped cages with no room for mobility. Their lifespan is cut in half. Some chicken farmers have caught on to the growing concern and are raising cage-free chicken.

Pigs show fertility problems after eating GMO BT corn. A study claimed that when the pigs switched over to regular corn the problem went away.

Beef is another controversial topic. Cattle farmers use estradiol and progestin. These hormones increase the weight of the cattle before they are slaughtered. Because of these synthetic hormones, U.S. beef is banned in Europe. Scientists believe there is a link to breast cancer. In Europe a fine is paid because of their refusal to buy U.S. beef.

What is Bt/Bt toxin (Bacillus Thuringiensis)?
Bt is used to modify the plants into resisting the Round-Up, or more specifically, glyphosate.

The plants make a protein that internally protects them from insects. The insects that the plant/crop is protected from are corn borers, tobacco budworm, cotton bollworm, pink bollworm and the Colorado potato beetle.

When the cells of the plant are modified with Bt, they produce pesticides that make an insect's stomach burst after they try eating the plant. Some scientists believe it is not safe for humans. The seeds are usually called "Round-up ready" and the plants they produce are usually called "Bt corn" or "Bt soy", etc.

The genes that are inserted into the plants are passed into the animals and humans who eat them. In other words, washing the plants doesn't get rid of the residue of the pesticides-it becomes part of the plant's DNA. For example, genes inserted into soy will transfer into the DNA of bacteria that live inside of humans. Toxic insecticide produced by GM corn was found in the blood of pregnant women and then found in the blood of their babies.

How Can You Avoid Eating GMOs?

You can't-well, it's next to impossible. Monsanto and other corporations who produce GMO seeds do not have to include the modification on the label in the U.S. This fact is something that Monsanto has lobbied hard to not happen. Many GMOs are found in ready-made processed food, restaurants, and products that contain corn or soy as an ingredient.

The United Kingdom attributes GMO soy to the 50% allergy increase. Altered DNA changes the protein. In the U.K., GMO potatoes were under fire because they showed retarded development inside of organs and immune system problems.

Some scientists believe GMOs cause anti-social behavior and anxiety. In Appleton, Wisconsin a school removed all GMO foods from the cafeteria. Reportedly, they have had a huge reduction in behavioral problems.

Are there any whistle blowers?

In the U.K. Dr. Arpod Putsai's research found the negative side of GMOs in GMO potatoes. He once supported GMOs, but changed his mind while researching GMO safety in potatoes at the Rowett Institute. His findings suggested that modified potatoes seemed to retard the development in rat organs along with creating problems in the rats' immune system. Not willing to look the other way, he publicly expressed his concerns on a television show.

Dr. Putsai's study set off many alarms, especially with Prime Minister Tony Blair, a well-known cheerleader for bio-tech food. The day after the television interview Dr. Putsai was suspended from Rowett Institute with a gag order in place.

There was a silver lining to Dr. Putsai's candidness. Months later the gag order was lifted and Europeans, growing more and more suspicious of GMOs, used their consumer power to excise GMOs from all supermarkets.

In the U.S. Ignacio Chapela, a Berkeley professor, published evidence about GM corn that cross-pollinated with corn crops in Mexico. His biggest concern was the extinction of non-GMO corn. He was smeared all over a biotech forum website. Scientists demanded that he retract his study.

Before the article was released, Under-Secretary of Agriculture Victor Villalobos wrote the scientist an angry letter accusing him of doing "incalculable damage" to Mexico's agriculture. Chapela proudly displayed the letter on his desk and published his findings regardless of upsetting Mexico. The threats from the Mexican government continued, but Chapela would not back down.

Dr. Chapela didn't stop with Mexican corn. He publically opposed Berkeley for taking $50,000 grant from Novartis, a Big-Pharma company. The money would give Novartis first look on the bio-tech/GMO research. Chapela believed that Novartis was trying to buy the university so that current and future study results would validate Novartis's products. Dr. Chapela's tenure was denied for years.

rBGH (Recombinant Bovine Growth Hormone): What is it?

It's a man-made hormone that increases milk production in dairy cows. The FDA approved rBGH in 1993. The EU, Canada, and other countries ban it because of health concerns. Monsanto sells rBGH. They allegedly tried to bribe Canadian officials with a million dollars or more into legalizing it. Once "caught", Monsanto claimed the 'offering' was meant for research.

Dr. Margaret Miller, a researcher for Monsanto, created the hormone. Later, she was later hired onto the FDA where she took part in approving it. Michael Taylor, the number two at FDA, helped keep the hormone off of the ingredient labels.

This hormone stimulates another hormone known as IGF-1. The possible health effects range. One of the big problems is the udder infections that arise once the cows are injected with rBGH. The udder infections are treated with antibiotics. The antibiotics lead to resistant bacteria inside of the cows. This could also lead to human resistance to antibiotics. When a scientist modifies an organism, he/she has to add a promoter to activate the gene. The promoter can also unintentionally activate other genes. Promoters can transfer into humans' gut bacteria. Doctors worry about the long-term effects.

The milk produced from rBGH cows has higher levels of IGF-1. Several studies have found that high IGF-1 levels help some types of cells grow and influence the development of cancer, specifically prostate (4X more likely), breast (7X more likely), and colorectal. However, other studies show no connection. So which is it- harmful or safe? Both sides have their results that "prove" what they want proved. Other countries back the "causes cancer" side of the issue by banning it.

Top retailers such as Walmart, Starbucks, Kroger's, and many more won't sell dairy with this hormone. Monsanto sold their rBGH business to Eli Lilly's Elanco, a big-pharma corporation.

What about the heavy use of <u>antibiotics</u> for dairy cows?

Penicillin, florfenicol, sulfamethazine, and sulfadimethoxine are some of the common antibiotics given to dairy cows when diagnosed with mastitis. The mastitis results from the inflammation of the cow's udder. If the mastitis gets to an uncontrollable level, then the dairy cow is slaughtered

One of the main problems with antibiotics is the length of time the cows are on the drug. In addition, lactating cows are not supposed to take penicillin, but this 'rule' is half-heartedly followed. Doctors worry that constant human consumption of milk will build an immunity to antibiotics. Antibiotics are also blamed for the spike in allergies across the nation.

Comment [C]:

Phenylbutazone, a non-steroidal anti-inflammatory, is also used for udder and uterine infections. This drug is linked with anemia, leukopenia, agranulocytosis, and thrombocytopenia. In 2003 this drug was banned by the FDA but still shows up in random samples of dairy cows.

Why do people want raw milk?

Pasteurized milk has the name Pasteur in it. It was Louis Pasteur who discovered harmful bacteria in raw milk. By heating the milk for a

75

certain amount of time, bacteria responsible for listeriosis, typhoid fever, TB, diphtheria, and brucellosis are killed.

So why would one want to risk getting sick off of raw milk? Many raw milk drinkers don't trust the government and their health warnings. They are especially leery over processed milk and processed foods in general. Raw milk drinkers believe that the dairy cows used for raw milk are cleaner than the dairy cows used for pasteurized milk. They also believe that raw milk helps with digestion and intestinal problems, allergies, heart disease, acne, and cancer. It was the only way people drank milk before Pasteur came along, so what's the big deal? The FDA only increases raw milk drinkers' fears by banning the sale of raw milk for human consumption across state lines.

Major GMO crops are soy, corn, cotton, canola, papaya and zucchini. rGBH is also considered one of the biggest GMOs sold to the public. Where does wheat fit in?

GM wheat is not patented yet. Monsanto is working hard to perfect this main crop. They are currently in the early development stage. Monsanto believes it will be ready for FDA approval in a couple of years. It will be Round-Up resistant like other GMO crops.

How do other countries feel about GMO food?

Here is a recent list from *The Nation* of countries that completely or partially banned GMOs.

Switzerland, Australia, Austria, China, India, France, Germany, Hungary, Luxembourg, Greece, Bulgaria, Poland, Italy, Mexico and Russia. China does not grow GMOs, but they do import some GMO crops. With the world's largest population of 1.351 billion people, many scientists believe they need to produce GM crops for a larger domestic food supply. China's people and leaders are very leery despite having to rely on other countries' imports for food.

Sixty other countries have restrictions on GM crops. Why? For the same reasons so many Americans are opposed to GM crops. Unlike America, their governments aren't indebted to Big-

Agri. Many buy into the argument that once the genes are altered then so is the nutritional value of the crops. Cross pollination of GMOs mixing with organic crops is also a concern. Some believe that GMOs can ruin species of bugs and animals. On the other hand, some believe that bugs are becoming resistant to the crops, creating a superbug which of course will require more herbicide.

Are animals genetically modified?

Yes and no. GM salmon is in the process of developing. These salmon are called Franken-fish. Most salmon take 30 months to mature while the genetically modified salmon take about half the time. A company called AquaBounty in Massachusetts combine traits from other fish to create this gigantic version of salmon.

http://www.dailymail.co.uk/news/article-2517137/The-Frankenfish-GM-super-salmon-muscling-way-plate.html

Some animals not used for food are genetically modified for pharmaceutical purposes. And then there is cloning such as the success of Dolly the famous sheep. Eastern nations clone pets for heart-broken pet owners.

Israel has developed the featherless chicken. This breed is meant to save money and time. This chicken is a combination of two kinds of chicken interbred. The feathers gave protection from parasites and weather. Will the new breed adapt without feathers?

Tilapia are genetically modified for size and a shortened time to reach maturity. Males are preferred because female tilapia do not get as big while protecting their eggs.

What about GMO contamination in meat?
Crops are grown with GM seeds and livestock eat the crops, therefore the livestock are contaminated. Once slaughtered, is the meat contaminated?

You are what you eat. Most animals are fed GMO feed, usually soy. Sixty to ninety percent of all soy is genetically modified. U.S. regulation claims that GM fed animals do not carry a GM label because the feed is broken down during the animals' digestion. Supposedly, it is undetected.

GM DNA was found in blood, organs, and milk of goats. Goats eat GM soy. The feed allegedly causes lactic dehydrogenase (enzyme) to elevate which causes problems during immune reactions. Bt toxin protein can be found in pregnant women and their fetuses.

The additives in ham and sausage are genetically modified. Ascorbic acid keeps the color of sausage. Glutamate gives flavor. Enzymes improve smell. Bacon, a food under fire for all kinds of reasons, is currently being modified with genes from spinach in order to change saturated fat found in the meat into unsaturated fat. These pigs are called Popeye pigs.

Most livestock are fed GMO food, but if given a choice, they tend to prefer organic food. One farmer (Fonder) conducted a study on five different occasions. He fed squirrels both organic and GMO corn. The results were the same each time. The squirrels preferred the organic food was consumed first and then the squirrels would eat the GMO corn.

Chapter Four

Most Harmful Chemicals in Food

There are three thousand chemicals found in the American food supply. As previously mentioned in this book, the FDA was created to protect consumers against harmful products in food, beverages, and cosmetics. Many of the people who serve the FDA have come from the same companies that are looking for FDA approval. The conflict of interest is not widely publicized for obvious reasons. This chapter lists some of the most harmful FDA approved chemicals on the market.

Aspartame: This artificial sweetener is found in many sugar-free products. It's made of methanol, phenylalanine and aspartic acid. It's sold under brand names such as Equal and NutraSweet and has 0 calories. It was discovered in the 1980's and meant to replace saccharin, another sweetener found in Tab cola that has links to cancer.

Aspartame was tested on rats. The results were very questionable. Cancerous brain tumors, fibromyalgia, Multiple Sclerosis, diabetes, and depression are linked to changes in serotonin levels. This sweetener has links to these diseases.

Ironically, many diabetics use aspartame as a substitute for sugar. It aggravates retinopathy, cataracts, neuropathy and gastro paresis. Some diabetics have had convulsions from aspartame commonly mistaken for insulin reactions.

Many people drink beverages with aspartame to control weight. Nutritionists believe that aspartame increases hunger because it causes spikes in insulin levels and forces the body to store glucose as fat. Aspartame also inhibits serotonin levels, preventing the brain from transmitting a full feeling in the stomach.

Many believe aspartame is linked to birth defects. It acts as an excitotoxin that kills or damages cells in the nervous system which can cause brain damage.

Aspartame is also associated with memory loss.

Why is aspartame FDA approved?

Aspartame was originally rejected by the FDA. Donald Rumsfeld, the former head of Searle, called in a favor. President Ronald Reagan fired the head of the FDA and installed a new FDA head who was friendly to Searle. On a side note, Monsanto bought Searle shortly afterward.

Besides the links to many diseases, aspartame comes from the feces of GM E. coli bacteria. Our diet drinks use genetically modified feces as a main ingredient.

High Fructose Corn Syrup (HFCS): This syrup is made from GMO corn and then processed with GMO enzymes. It's composed of fructose and glucose and used as a preservative and sweetener in food. Many believe that it leads to obesity and diabetes as well as heart disease. Some studies have tested HFCS and found mercury in half of their samples.

Yellow #5/tartrazine: This chemical dye is used in food, drugs, and cosmetics. It's made from coal tar/benzene and may contain lead and arsenic in it. It's found in soft drinks, cotton candy, pudding, corn chips, cereal, pickles, cakes, pastries, Twinkies, sports drinks, and many kinds of processed food. It's also found in cosmetics, hair products, hand sanitizer, vitamins, antacids, and some prescription drugs. Many disorders and diseases are associated with tartrazine such as depression, cancer, asthma, ADD, lupus, skin discoloration, obesity, sterility, and more.

Yellow #6: This is the third most often used chemical in food coloring. It's common in candy, gelatin, bakery, and sausages. It is linked with adrenal gland and kidney tumors.

Blue #1 and Blue #2: Blue one is used to color candy, beverages, and bakery. It may cause cancer. Blue 2 is found in pet food, beverages, and candy. It causes brain tumors in mice.

Red #3: This is used to color candy, bakery, and cherries in fruit cocktail. It causes thyroid tumors in rats and may cause them in humans.

Titanium Dioxide: This is a paint pigment that is used to make things whiter. It sometimes contains lead. It's used in coffee creamers, cake icing, and salad dressing. It is also found in sunscreen. Although it is very effective in blocking harmful sun rays, many question if it is dangerous once absorbed into the skin.

Caramel Coloring (4-Mel): It's a sugar compound heated together with ammonium compounds, acids or alkalis. It gives soft drinks a dark brown color and looks like baked goods have cocoa in them. The ammonia that is used to process caramel coloring is linked with cancer (lung, liver, thyroid, and leukemia).

In certain soft drinks (Pepsico is mentioned), caramel coloring exceeds amounts that are considered to be "safe". There are no warnings on the labels.

Cochineal Extract and Carmine: These are red colorings that come from the cochineal insect. These insects are boiled, dried, and mixed to make a dye that is used in candy, yogurt, coffee drinks such as Starbucks' Frappucinos, ice cream, drugs, and cosmetics. This insect was originally used by Aztecs for dying fabric red. About 70,000 insects produce one pound of dye. This dye is traded all over the world.

It's listed as an artificial coloring or "color added" so the consumer can't tell if it's in the food that he/she is buying. Some people are allergic to this bug and can break out in hives and anaphylactic shock.

Bromine/Brominated Vegetable Oil (BVO): It's a natural element found in the earth and seawater. It can be used in place of chlorine in swimming pools. , Bromine is most commonly used as a fire retardant for furniture, carpeting, car seats, and mattresses.

Brominated vegetable oil is used in soft drinks such as Mountain Dew and Gatorade. Its main purpose is to give the beverages a slightly cloudy appearance. It's a stabilizer that keeps citric oil from separating.

Bromine or bromine mixed with vegetable oil builds in human tissue and linked with cancer, myocardial degeneration, and fatty liver. Those who have binged on drinks that contain BVO have reported skin lesions, memory loss, and nerve disorders.

Bromine is banned as a food additive in the EU, Union India, Nepal, Canada, Brazil, and Japan. Gatorade is sold in those countries, but the recipe is aligned with law. The million dollar question: *Why can't the recipe be modified in the United States?*

Potassium bromate (brominated flour): This chemical improves the texture and rising in dough used for bread. Again, this chemical is banned in several countries including China. Who would have thought China has more sophisticated food standards than the U.S., but in some cases they do.

This chemical causes cancer in rats and is toxic to human kidneys. It's found in flatbreads, wraps (for sandwiches), and bread. Some corporate bakeries such as Pepperidge Farm,

Pillsbury, and Entenmann's have switched over to a safer flour, but many supermarket chains that sell baked goods still use potassium bromate. Some flour brands like Gold Medal have a few products that contain potassium bromate. Whole Foods refuses to sell anything with potassium bromate in it. Although it is commonly used in pizza dough, Pizza Hut and Domino's Pizza don't use it.

Azodicarbonamide: This chemical is used as a blowing agent in the manufacturing of rubbers and pipes, and used in making synthetic leather and foam plastic. It's also used as a food additive that bleaches and improves flour. It's found in sandwich bread, doughnuts, bagels, chewing gum, and fast-food hamburger buns from McDonald's and Burger King. It's banned in Australia and EU. Singapore has a law that will imprison a baker/corporation for up to fifteen years and fine up to $450,000 if caught using this chemical, yet the U.S. eats it up by the truckload. The main health concern related to Azodicarbonamide has to do with respiratory sensitizer. In short, some believe it causes allergies and asthma.

Propylene glycol alginate (E405): This food additive is used as an emulsifier, thickener, and stabilizer. It comes from alginic acid combined with propylene glycol. It's found in antifreeze and airport runway de-icers. It is most commonly found in salad dressings, yogurt, and soft drinks. It's suspected of causing liver and kidney diseases and seizures in children.

Butylated Hydroxyanisole (BHA), Butylated Hydroxytoluene (BHT): BHT is found in jet fuel and embalming fluid. These chemicals are a common preservative used in some fats and oils that are found in food, drugs, and cosmetics. They are also commonly found in processed butter, meat, cereal, gum, vitamins, baked goods, dehydrated potatoes, and beer. California considers BHA a carcinogen and BHT is linked with liver enlargement.

Propyl Gallate: This preservative is often used in conjunction with BHA and BHT. It's a preservative used to prevent fats and oils from spoiling and commonly found in meat products, potato sticks, chicken soups, and gum. It is linked with cancer.

Polysorbate 60: This chemical is made from corn, palm oil and petroleum. It won't spoil. Baked goods, junk food, and dairy products use this as an ingredient. It's also found in skin care products. It's linked with cancer.

MSG-monosodium glutamate: This food additive is used as a flavor enhancer. It doesn't have any flavor, but will produce flavor once added to food. It's commonly found in Chinese food, Campbell's soup, Doritos, Cheetos, Hamburger Helper, canned gravy, and frozen dinners.

The average supermarket shopper has half of her/his cart filled with MSG products. It's also found in some household cleaners. Some of the health risks include brain damage, allergies, diabetes, nausea, depression, obesity, ADD, asthma, and memory loss. It has been implicated in the most serious of diseases such as Lou Gehrig's Disease, MS, Parkinson's, and Alzheimer's. MSG has addictive properties that keep the eater coming back for more.

Sodium Nitrate/Sodium Nitrite: Sodium Nitrate is a type of salt that can be found in Chile or Peru. It can also be created in a lab. Sodium Nitrite is also a salt, but created in a lab during a chemical reaction. Sodium Nitrate breaks down into Sodium Nitrite. To spare you the chemistry lesson (and myself as a writer), these two have subtle differences, but are the same species in hazardous food additives. Sodium nitrate was originally used to preserve meat and prevent botulism. Today it is dyed pink and used as a preservative found in processed meats such as bacon, canned meat, and lunchmeat from the deli. When sodium nitrite is overcooked, the new chemical from the reaction is nitrosamines, a carcinogen. In short, these chemicals are linked with cancer.

Trans Fats: Saturated fats will raise one's cholesterol level, but trans fats do even more damage by wiping out the HDL (good cholesterol) in the body, making the consumer very vulnerable to heart disease. Trans fats promote obesity. They are found in chips, hamburgers, popcorn, biscuits, and all kinds of junk food.

Olestra: This fake fat is found in products that are advertised as being healthy and low fat. It is not cancerous in itself, but becomes cancerous when it binds with vitamins A, D, E, and K which boost immunity to cancer. Many consumers have reported stomach problems.

Sulfites: These are preservatives used in dried fruits, cookies, crackers, and cereals. They are created naturally during the fermentation of beer and wine. In 1984 the FDA banned sulfites to be added in raw foods set in salad bars. They are connected with asthma.

Acesulfame-K: This artificial sweetener is two hundred times sweeter than sugar. When it breaks down in the digestive system, it forms acetoacetamide, a chemical that affects the thyroid in animals. It's used in baked goods, gum, desserts, and soft drinks. This chemical is linked with cancer.

Castoreum: This is extracted from beavers' anal glands. Beavers mix this with their urine to mark their territories. It's used to make berry or vanilla pudding, gelatin, and yogurt. Again, it's not listed as an ingredient and called "natural flavorings". Not sure of health risks, but it's disgusting.

Sulphates: These chemicals are found in shampoos and soaps. They produce lather which strips away dirt and grease. One of the problems is that they also strip away natural oils, causing hair and skin to dry out and become irritated. In some cases one may lose her/his hair. Studies may link sulphates to cancer. Consumers are beginning to demand sulphate-free shampoos.

Paraben: These preservatives (methylparaben, ethylparaben, propylparaben, butylparaben and isobutylparaben) stop fungus and bacteria from growing in many cosmetics. Parabens are most commonly found in lotions and hair products, replacing formaldehyde as the preservative. Although there is no proof that parabens cause cancer, there are important links that question safety. Researcher Philippa Darbre of the University of Reading in England published a ground-breaking study that found parabens in eighteen out of twenty samples of tissue from breast cancer cells. This may be one of the reasons that "paraben free" labels are popping up in the beauty section of big box and department stores.

Aluminum: This metal is found in deodorant. Many believe the aluminum which blocks sweat is absorbed into the skin and interferes with estrogen, causing cancerous results. Aluminum deposits are often found inside of the breast when doctors cut in during a mastectomy.

Canola Oil: Most canola oil is genetically modified. Interestingly, it doesn't come from anything. Canola stands for Canadian oil low acid. Production begins with the rapeseed plant, a plant from the mustard family. This oil works well for candles, soaps, make-up, biofuel, and lubricants.

Studies link canola oil to kidney and liver problems along with heart lesions. Other problems such as cancer and blood platelet abnormalities are also linked to canola oil.

MDF (medium density fiberboard): Although not a food or cosmetic, this is another item on the very long list of health hazards. MDF is used in construction for moldings, kitchen cabinets, floors, and anything that needs to look like wood. It's about 1/10th the price of real wood. There are many articles that claim that MDF is perfectly safe and just as many that claim that MDF is harmful. Supposedly, MDF manufacturers have paid attention to concerned consumers, using nontoxic chemicals over the previously used formaldehyde.

These chemicals suggest a theme of disease. Cancer, MS, asthma, ADD/ADHD, depression, etc. are linked with the chemicals that are put inside of our food and toiletries. To take it one step further, who benefits when we are sick? Big Pharma. The new food chain: seeds are engineered by Big-Agri/Food, animals eat the seeds, and we eat the seeds and animals, we get sick, then we take drugs from Big Pharma...And round and round it goes. So what's the alternative?

Chapter Five

Organics

In summary, animal studies have linked GMO food to organ damage, gastrointestinal and immune disorders, accelerated aging, and infertility. Some countries believe it might be the cause to allergies. Some scientists are also testing it for a possible connection to autism, ADD, and some emotional disorders. Proof is controversial. Those who say negative things about GMO food are discredited. Those who are supposed to protect us (FDA and USDA) have conflicted interests. Meanwhile, other countries have stricter laws regarding types and amounts of GMO crops that are allowed into the country. You want to play it safe? Organic food needs a second look.

Organic food is a type of food that is grown in compliance to USDA standards. If one wants to grow or raise an organic product, then natural pesticides are used, more work like crop rotation is required, and seeds and/or livestock are not genetically modified. Organic crops cannot be fertilized with toxic sewage sludge or coal waste. They cannot be irrigated with E. coli contaminated sewage water. Organic animals must be fed organic food free of hormones, GM vaccines, and antibiotics and have access to pastures for grazing. They cannot be caged up for long periods of time.

To earn the organic USDA label, an organic product has to be considered 95% organic. If a farmer "cheats", claiming organic when not, then there is a $10,000 violation. Organic food producers must keep meticulous records for everything. They are under constant governmental scrutiny.

Organic food is **almost always more expensive than conventional food. Conventional (GMO) farmers are granted subsidies while organic farmers are put on the defense, paying fees to prove their food is organic.** Much more labor is needed before the organic food hits the food stands. For example, the cost of a GM apple is equally split into labor, interest, and taxes. It also lasts longer on the shelf so less waste and more profit. The cost of an organic apple consists of mostly labor and start-up materials.

A $25 million dollar four year study in the EU states that organic fruits or vegetables have up to 50% antioxidants, vitamins, and minerals. Organic foods taste better and are safer for babies. The average newborn has two hundred toxins and carcinogens in her/his body. Organic food might even be considered a necessity for babies.

Organic food supposedly reduces the risk of CJD (Creutzfeldt-Jakob) which is the human form of Mad Cow Disease. Organic food is also said to reduce the effects of Alzheimer's disease. Organic food contains less bacteria. Organic chicken is free of salmonella.

Organic food is not irradiated. The EPA's (www.epa.gov) definition is as follows:

Food irradiation is a technology for controlling spoilage and eliminating food-borne pathogens, such as salmonella. The result is similar to conventional pasteurization and is often called "cold pasteurization" or "irradiation pasteurization." Like pasteurization, irradiation kills bacteria and other pathogens that could otherwise result in spoilage or food poisoning. The fundamental difference between the two methods is the source of the energy they rely on to destroy the microbes. While conventional pasteurization relies on heat, irradiation relies on the energy of ionizing radiation. The FDA emphasizes that no preservation method is a substitute for safe food handling procedures.

Besides the healthier component, organics are also better for the environment, especially soil and water. Organic farming uses fifty percent less energy than conventional farming.

Organic food consumption has become a multi-billion dollar business. In 2012 organic foods reached $28 billion in the U.S., an 11% jump from 2011. Organics are also growing in household products and cosmetics. Seventy percent of Americans buy organic occasionally and one-fourth of Americans buy every week.

Walmart has broken into the organic business, promising to stock shelves with organics at a much lower price than other grocery stores. They have already installed their Wild Oats line of organic food in four thousand stores. If proven successful, Walmart will soon supply every store with their Wild Oats food line while charging much more affordable prices than their competitors.

Organics are expensive but in the long run, are they cheaper than the health problems that conventional food might cause? Food for thought. If you are on a budget like most of the country, here is a list of foods that matter the most when going organic.

Peaches

Strawberries

Nectarines

Potatoes

Lettuce

Apples

Grapes

Spinach

Celery

Pears

Bell peppers

Cherries

Milk (At the very least, milk that is hormone free)

Comment [C]:

Foods with heavy rinds like bananas, grapefruit or oranges aren't as much of a concern.

Natural food: To be considered natural, the food must have no artificial ingredients, coloring, or chemical preservatives. It must be minimally processed (Processed food is a physical or chemical treatment that changes the original food). Natural food is often confused with organic food, but they are not the same thing.

As people become more educated about food, the organic business continues to explode. Who owns and sells organic food? Some of the big names involved in buying out mid-sized organic food businesses are Coca-Cola, Campbell, Pepsi, Nestle, and Coors-Millers. Allegedly, the quality of the food changes once the company is bought out.

Dr. Howard, a researcher from Michigan State University, has been tracking organic business takeover for years. He believes that big corporations are putting cheaper ingredients in their newly acquired products to increase their profit margins. He uses several examples such as Silk Soymilk that was acquired by Dean Foods. He also notes that many of these companies politically contribute to politicians with anti-environment agendas. Coca-Cola for example gave more than one million dollars to block GMO labeling in California.

Chapter Six

Natural Remedies

Pills and processed foods are becoming ingrained in the American lifestyle. There are ways to break free. This chapter touches on the healing powers of certain foods, vitamins, and herbs. These natural products cannot be monopolized through a patent and are open for all to consume. Alternative medicine is worth looking at.

The U.S. is unique to other parts of the world. Because of our strong lobby for natural dietary supplements, we still do not abide by the European Codex Alimentarius or at least not yet. DSHEA (Dietary Supplement Health and Education Act of 1994) protects the health supplement sellers so far. However, this situation is constantly being tested by the pharmaceutical industry.

In the E.U., hundreds of vitamins are restricted or banned. High dose vitamins are prohibited and only low doses of vitamins are available. The vitamin business is being taken over by Big Pharma to ensure "safety" of the product. Supposedly, E.U. officials fear that vitamins will not be taken safely and want them harmonized with the food code.

If vitamins become something that one needs a prescription for, then their price will rise to three or four times of what they cost when sold over-the-counter. This becomes a new market with more profits for Big Pharma. For example, in France it is illegal to sell Vitamin C in dosages over 200 mg (1000 mg is RDA). Great Britain has two hundred and fifty banned vitamins, including Vitamin C and B6. Most of Europe has banned chromium, picolinate, yeast, lysine, and selenium. Europe considers vitamins to be classified as drugs.

Europe in general has very different vitamin laws than the U.S. Imported fortified foods require a governmental approval. This costs roughly $1700 per product for stores to have permission to sell. The E.U. is suspicious of fortified foods, claiming that too many vitamins and minerals can be toxic. This partly explains the restrictions. **Kellogg, an American cereal maker,** had eighteen products denied because of iron, calcium, vitamin B, and other supplements.

Many American natural supplement dealers fear that U.S. will cave and adhere to the same European set of laws pertaining to vitamins and minerals. So far, grass roots lobbies have protected these retailers and vitamin distributors, but most feel it is just a matter of time.

Herbs are used for medication, but are considered as food and not medicine by the FDA (at least so far). They are not subject to the scrutiny of pharmaceuticals. Because of this, they cannot make any health claims on medical conditions. For instance, St. John's Wort supposedly helps depression, but they cannot put that on label. Instead, the manufacturer has to either leave any claims off of the label or state something like "enhances mood."

Some vitamins and minerals have preventative and healing properties that need closer examination. My research on this subject was endless. There are at least five thousand herbs in the world. An herbalist might have expertise in up to thousand herbs. A few herbs, vitamins, and minerals kept coming up on a multitude of websites, making them worthy to mention for the purposes of this book.

Flaxseed: This is the new "it" food, although its benefits have been known since 3000 B.C. King Charlemagne passed a law requiring his citizens to eat it. It can naturally be found in cereals and grains or purchased in the vitamin/mineral/herbal section of any drug store. It has many healthy components, especially Omega-3 essential fatty acids, lignans, and fiber. There are many links that claim flaxseed fights cancer, stroke, heart disease, and diabetes.

Fish Oil: This oil has alpha-linoleic acid (ALA), eicosapentaenoic acid (EPA), and docosahexaenoic acid (DHA) and most commonly found in salmon along with avocados, walnuts, olive oil, and tofu. This oil is known for helping to combat heart disease. Fish oil can be purchased in pill form. Krill oil has a lower concentration in these important acids.

Echinacea: Also called the cone flower, Echinacea is an herb. All parts of the flower are used to make medicine for colds, yeast infections, gum disease, herpes, septicemia (blood infection), strep, syphilis, and many other infections and/or diseases. It helps with chronic fatigue, ADHD, rattlesnake bites, bee stings, and eczema. Talk about versatility! The Great Plains Indians used Echinacea for many purposes. Unfortunately, anti-biotics have replaced Echinacea in the medical world, but one can buy it in juices or tablets.

Glucosamine: This is a liquid substance found in fluid around human joints, animal bones, marrow, shellfish and fungi. It works small miracles for people with arthritis or join pain because it builds cartilage. It also works for dogs with arthritis problems.

Glucosamine might help MS patients as well. Dr. Michael Demetriou's article in The Journal of Biological Chemistry states that this supplement corrects genetic defects of the growth and function of abnormal T-cells. It's the T-cells that make the MS patient's immune system attack itself. His study used mice with a mock MS disease that had problems with walking. Once the mice were given the glucosamine, their T-cell hyperactivity was suppressed and their walking problems were reversed. Another research team from Jefferson Medical College found that glucosamine delayed MS symptoms in an animal experiment.

Rose: This is usually sold as an oil that one inhales. Rose petals are supposed to help with menstrual cramps, depression, allergies, asthma, and headaches.

Ginger: This is usually used for food or tea, but also can be taken as a capsule. It helps with digestion, nausea, and motion sickness.

Ginseng: This herb is typically grown in the northern hemisphere with some exception. It can be used for several diseases and ailments. Studies have proved its ability to lower glucose levels in Type 2 Diabetes. The herb also works as an aphrodisiac, hair regrowth product, skin product, weight loss aid, premenstrual syndrome aid, cancer tumor growth inhibitor, and solution to Erectile Dysfunction. Side effects are minimal to none. This herb can be taken by tea, pill, or used as a spice for many dishes.

Gingko: This herb is also known as the maidenhair tree and is considered to be a living fossil. Gingko is known to help dementia, anxiety, and schizophrenia. It might also help autism, ADD/ADHD, dyslexia, kidney disease, MS, anti-aging, mental performance as a whole, blood pressure, depression, cancer, and many other problems.

Garlic: This herb is the one of the best for heart disease related issues. It improves cholesterol levels and lowers blood pressure. The E.U. classifies garlic as both foodstuffs and medicine. There are strict laws concerning the purchase of garlic in about half of Europe.

Dandelion: This weed works miracles. It works as a cleanser, helps diabetes, treats acne, anemia, cancer, PMS, and urinary issues.

Curry Powder/Turmeric: This is a mixture that usually contains turmeric, fenugreek, coriander, ginger, cinnamon, cayenne pepper, and/or cardamom. Turmeric studies suggest that this spice prevents spikes in blood sugar which contributes to diabetes. Curcumin, turmeric's active compound, works much like rosiglitazone, a diabetes drug. Curcumin is also considered a cancer-preventative and also has the ability to stop cancer from the onset. Curcumin is being developed into a natural anticancer drug. Curry powder may also lower cholesterol and prevent cholesterol gallstones. The coriander in the curry powder may help detoxify the body and improve testosterone levels and low sperm count. Curcumin when taken with Vitamin D3 can also prevent Alzheimer's disease. It also works as an anti-inflammatory drug for arthritis. If that's not enough, it also wards off osteoporosis.

St. John's Wort: A plant with yellow flowers that grows wild. It's been used for centuries for depression.

Stinging Nettle: This plant is proven to be effective with allergies, especially hay fever. It is also used for eczema, arthritis, urinary problems, and gout.

Vitamin D3: No, this is not an herb, but needed to be added to this list because of its important healing properties. This is also called the sunshine drug and is essential in preventing, improving, and possibly curing several diseases. Best-selling author Jeff Bowles used himself as a guinea pig by consuming huge amounts of Vitamin D3. His self-experiment and research has gotten much attention. Vitamin D3 may be able to prevent, help, and maybe even cure MS, obesity, erectile dysfunction, Alzheimer's disease, foot funguses, several cancers, lethargy, and much more. This vitamin deserves a place on everyone's shelf.

As mentioned previously, vitamins are freely sold in the U.S. as of now, but are either banned from the shelves or highly diluted in potency in the E.U. Like vitamins, herbs have their boundaries. Despite age-old usage for medicine in many cultures, some governments have banned them from public consumption and even tried to patent them for profit.

The E.U. has passed a series of directives that fall under Napoleonic law-guilty until proven innocent. In the world of herbs, this means the herb is banned unless it is specifically allowed. Restrictions have narrowed to an almost impossible level for over-the-counter herbs. Special licensing is required for retail. Only fifty herbs have "passed" the E.U. standards for legal sales.

Is it possible to patent an herb?

As far as the U.S. goes, no, not yet. Big Pharma is certainly trying and will almost certainly succeed as time goes by. As of the here and now, herbs cannot be patented, just copied. A scientist can take the chemicals that heal from an herb, tinker with the molecular structure just enough so that it is officially different, and then patent the product as a drug for profit. By the way, the leading cause of death in the U.S. is adverse drug reactions.

Big Pharma will probably continue to try and patent herbs, waiting for their governmental puppets to pass the right legislation to set them up. For example, Nestle, known for the candy and other food products, seeks a patent for the fennel flower which is also known as black seed or black cumin. This herb prevents food allergies. Big Pharma has feverishly tried to patent turmeric but has so far failed.

Patenting herbs brings back the subject of bio-piracy mentioned earlier in the book. Bio-piracy is a problem. Besides Fennel Flower and Turmeric, Neem (an herb with fungicidal properties), Basmati (rice), rice in general (22,972 varieties from India), and Pentadiplandra brazzeana (African berry) have caught the interest of Big Pharma. The idea that a giant corporation can go into an indigenous land and "discover" plants that have been used by cultures for centuries is not only wrong, but immoral. What next? A patent on water? Can air be patented?

Chapter Seven

The Rise of Anti-Depressants

Why are prescriptions for anti-depressants (SSRIs) and other drugs like Ritalin sky-rocking?

The U.S. only comprises 5% of the world's population yet use 34% of prescription drugs. Many doctors believe the American society is over-diagnosed and over-drugged. Some go as far to say that ailments, emotional lows, and some behavioral disorders were invented to profit the industry.

Anti-depressants are the most prescribed medication in the United States. A study in the Archives of General Psychiatry reports that the present day use of anti-depressants has grown to 10.12%, almost double from 5.84% of 1996-2005. That equates to twenty-seven million Americans, some as young as six years old, taking SSRIs. Many believe that figure is too conservative with 25% of all Americans having some kind of a mental illness. A more recent study from 2006 to 2008 shows that 1 out of every ten Americans take SSRIs.

Australia estimates that 61% or thirteen million people take anti-depressants and one in five people have a mood disorder. U.K. has forty-six million citizens on some kind of anti-depressants.

Lexipro, Zoloft, Paxil, and Prozac are the most popular of the prescriptions. Therapy once pioneered by Sigmund Freud is being replaced with pills. These prescriptions are prescribed for major depression, anxiety, as well as situational depression. Some blame the increase of prescriptions on the insurance companies who are not as generous with psychologist/psychiatrist visits, preferring the more inexpensive pill-popping solution. One third of people with emotional problems were in some kind of therapy twenty years ago. That number has dwindled down to 20%. Some of the major side effects are sexual dysfunction, stomach problems, and withdrawal symptoms.

Cynical experts believe the increased usage of SSRIs has everything to do with expanding the criteria of the disorders. The DSM-V, the manual/list/dictionary/bible of all psychological disorders, keeps getting thicker. Many of its writers have ties to Big Pharma.

Who are taking these pills?

Everyone. However, there is one group of people who seem to be the exception-African Americans. Only 4.5% of African Americans are taking SSRIs, a number that was only 3.6% a decade earlier. Reports claim that of the 10-11% of the U.S. population who take the drugs, only one-third have true symptoms of major depression. Females are two and half times more likely to take them over males. One-quarter of all women between the ages of forty through fifty-nine take anti-depressants. Less than one-third of anti-depressant users get them from a psychiatrist.

Are these prescriptions necessary? Or are we becoming a drugged-out nation along with our western counterparts?

To start with, one must examine who exactly is profiting off of this exponential problem. In 2008 the U.S. spent $26 billion on SSRIs. In that same year suicide was responsible for 1.5% or 36,035 deaths. Three years later plus an extra $3.7 billion (up to about $30,000 billion in SSRIs) suicide accounted for the same percentage of deaths-1.5%, taking 38,285 deaths. Obviously, these meds do not cure anything. However, many people swear that they help them cope with depression, making them invaluable.

So what's the catch?

SSRIs (selective serotonin reuptake inhibitors) have side effects. The ones that doctors, patients, and Big Pharma report are sexual dysfunction, weight gain, diarrhea, sleep disturbance, dizziness, nausea, lethargy, headache, anxiety, and agitation. These effects tend to happen early on and usually disappear as the body gets used to the drug. Magic pill? Some people swear these drugs have changed their lives for the better. But there is a dark side.

Some of the controversial emotional effects of long-term usage include hallucinations, suicide, brain damage, violent behavior in children and adults, more chronic depression, and drug dependency over empowerment of the patient. Other reports include gastro-intestinal bleeding and bone development problems. Expecting mothers might have a child predisposed to emotional disorders.

Prozac is known to cause anxiety and sedatives are usually prescribed with it. Eli Lily, a Big Pharma company that manufactures Prozac, found 21-28% of Prozac users experience anxiety. Eli Lilly fought hard to keep allegations that link the drug to murder and suicide out of the media.

Other disorders such as akathisia, Parkinson's, MS, dystonia, and dyskinesia are associated with SSRI usage. Akathisia, a disease that makes one restless, can cause aggression or suicide. Suicide rate is three times higher among SSRI users than nonusers.

With the recent Newtown massacre, SSRIs and violence are under even more scrutiny. In 1998, Brynn Hartman, wife of actor Phil Hartman, killed her husband and herself while taking Zoloft. Pfizer, Zoloft's manufacturer and one of the Big Pharma companies, was sued and settled with the family out of court.

In 2001, Wyoming, a man killed his wife, daughter, and granddaughter before killing himself. Paxil was blamed and Glaxo-Smith-Kline

(GSK) paid the family eight million dollars in a settlement.

About the same time Jay Johnston of Portland, Oregon, shot himself and didn't die, but blamed his doctor's prescription of Zoloft and Prozac. He sued his doctor for not monitoring him and won five million dollars. There was the infamous Columbine shooting when Dylan Klebold and Eric Harris killed eleven people. Harris was taking Luvox. Joseph Wesbecker in Virginia who was responsible for the 2007 Virginia Tech murders was also taking an anti-depressant. Then there was the 2008 Northern Illinois University shooting where Stephen Kazmierczak killed five students and wounded dozens more before killing himself. He was reportedly taking Paxil which now carries a black box warning on the label.

By 2004 widespread reports forced the FDA into action. They issued out black box warnings on some of the SSRI labels. A black box warning is the strongest warning on a prescription.

Many believe that soldiers are the perfect customer base for Big Pharma as they return from the Middle East diagnosed with post-traumatic stress syndrome (PTSD), and the U.S. government picks up the tab. Big Pharma finances the political campaigns for those who expand their business. The prison population is another potential customer base for SSRI marketing with Medicaid and Medicare paying their health costs.

SSRIs are also linked to birth defects. Expectant mothers were six times more likely to give have babies with pulmonary hypertension compared to mothers who did not take SSRIs. The newborn has a difficult time processing oxygen while breathing which can be fatal.

Some doctors claim that medications increase serotonin to an excitotoxin level or the level that the brain reacts when mentally ill. Again, 70 percent of all SSRI prescriptions come from physicians and not psychiatrists. The psychiatrists that do prescribe SSRIs once spent fifty minutes with each patient. Now they see on average three patients every hour.

SSRIs can zone out emotional responses to various situations, causing what's known as amotivational syndrome. In this syndrome the frontal lobes of the brain are damaged and the patient becomes apathetic, lethargic, isolated, and demotivated. The syndrome is controversial. Some doctors believe it does not exist, while others link unneeded prescriptions, cannabis, and adult ADD in part of the diagnosis.

The Institute for Safe Medication Practices published in the journal PloS One a report identifying 31 drugs that are disproportionately linked with reports of violent behavior. Here are the top ten:

10) **Desvenlafaxine (Pristiq)-Pfizer** This drug is 7.9 times more likely to be associated with violence than other drugs.

9) **Venlafaxine (Effexor)-Pfizer** Treats anxiety disorders. Effexor is 8.3 times more likely than other drugs to be related to violent behavior.

8) **Fluvoxamine (Luvox)-Jazz Pharmaceuticals** This SSRI is 8.4 times more likely than other medications to be linked with violence.

7) **Triazolam (Halcion)-Pfizer** This drug treats insomnia and is 8.7 times more likely to be linked with violence.

6) **Atomoxetine (Strattera)-Eli Lilly** An ADHD (attention-deficit hyperactivity disorder) drug that is 9 times more likely to be linked with violence compared to the average medication.

5) **Mefoquine (Lariam)-Hoffman La-Rouche** A treatment for malaria and has been linked with abnormal behavior for a long time. It is 9.5 times more likely to be linked with violence than other drugs.

4) **Amphetamines: (Various)** They are 9.6 times more likely to be linked to violence, compared to other drugs.

3 **Paroxetine (Paxil)-GlaxoSmithKline** It is 10.3 times more likely to be linked with violence compared to other drugs.

2) **Fluoxetine (Prozac)-Eli Lilly** One of the most well-known of the SSRIs. Prozac is 10.9 times more likely to be linked with violence in comparison with other medications.

1) **Varenicline (Chantix)-Pfizer** This is prescribed for those who want to quit smoking. It's 18 times more likely to be linked with violence compared to other drugs — by comparison, that

number for Xyban is 3.9 and just 1.9 for nicotine replacement.

Chapter Eight

ADD/ADHD: Is it a Real Disorder?

ADD stands for Attention Deficit Disorder and ADHD stands for Attention Deficit Hyperactivity Disorder. Children and adults who get diagnosed with this label have difficulty concentrating in school, work, and relationships. They are extremely impulsive and constantly interrupt. They have trouble waiting for anything, sitting still, and can be disorganized and forgetful. Sometimes their behavior is more internal, daydreaming at times when their focus is required.

About 11% of all children with a three to one boy to girl ratio have ADD or ADHD. Some parts of the U.S. report 20% of elementary children have the disorder. Roughly six million American children are currently taking medication for ADD or ADHD and that number is on the rise. The origin of the disease is still unknown. It's considered to be a neurobehavioral disorder and very treatable. The diagnosis hinges on observations of teachers, care-givers, family, and other important people who spend time with the child/person in question.

So how does a parent know their child has ADD/ADHD?

There is no X-Ray or blood test that provides evidence of the disease.

The DSM-V (the manual that gives disorders and diseases credibility) lists eighteen behaviors that a prospective ADD/ADHD candidate might have. If the teacher and parent check six or more of nine of these behaviors, the candidate has earned the label ADD/ADHD and the special education and drugs that go along with it. At least six million children have been diagnosed with ADD/ADHD.

The criterion was copied from an ADD forum and behavior symptoms:

A. Either (1) and/or (2).

1. Inattention: Six (or more) of the following symptoms have persisted for at least 6 months to a degree that is inconsistent with developmental level and that impact directly on social and academic/occupational activities. Note: for older adolescents and adults (ages 17 and older), only 4 symptoms are required. The symptoms are not due to oppositional behavior, defiance, hostility, or a failure to understand tasks or instructions.

(a) Often fails to give close attention to details or makes careless mistakes in schoolwork, at work, or during other activities (for example, overlooks or misses details, work is inaccurate).

(b) Often has difficulty sustaining attention in tasks or play activities (for example, has difficulty remaining focused during lectures, conversations, or reading lengthy writings).

(c) Often does not seem to listen when spoken to directly (mind seems elsewhere, even in the absence of any obvious distraction).

(d) Frequently does not follow through on instructions (starts tasks but quickly loses focus and is easily sidetracked, fails to finish schoolwork, household chores, or tasks in the workplace).

(e) Often has difficulty organizing tasks and activities. (Has difficulty managing sequential tasks and keeping materials and belongings in

order. Work is messy and disorganized. Has poor time management and tends to fail to meet deadlines.)

(f) Characteristically avoids, seems to dislike, and is reluctant to engage in tasks that require sustained mental effort (such as schoolwork or homework or, for older adolescents and adults, preparing reports, completing forms, or reviewing lengthy papers).

(g) Frequently loses objects necessary for tasks or activities (e.g., school assignments, pencils, books, tools, wallets, keys, paperwork, eyeglasses, or mobile telephones).

(h) Is often easily distracted by extraneous stimuli. (for older adolescents and adults may include unrelated thoughts.).

(i) Is often forgetful in daily activities, chores, and running errands (for older adolescents and adults, returning calls, paying bills, and keeping appointments).

2. Hyperactivity and Impulsivity: Six (or more) of the following symptoms have persisted for at least 6 months to a degree that is inconsistent with developmental level and that

impact directly on social and academic/occupational activities. Note: for older adolescents and adults (ages 17 and older), only 4 symptoms are required. The symptoms are not due to oppositional behavior, defiance, hostility, or a failure to understand tasks or instructions.

(a) Often fidgets or taps hands or feet or squirms in seat.

(b) Is often restless during activities when others are seated (may leave his or her place in the classroom, office or other workplace, or in other situations that require remaining seated).

(c) Often runs about or climbs on furniture and moves excessively in inappropriate situations. In adolescents or adults, may be limited to feeling restless or confined.

(d) Is often excessively loud or noisy during play, leisure, or social activities.

(e) Is often "on the go," acting as if "driven by a motor." Is uncomfortable being still for an extended time, as in restaurants, meetings, etc. Seen by others as being restless and difficult to keep up with.

(f) Often talks excessively.

(g) Often blurts out an answer before a question has been completed. Older adolescents or adults may complete people's sentences and "jump the gun" in conversations.

(h) Has difficulty waiting his or her turn or waiting in line.

(i) Often interrupts or intrudes on others (frequently butts into conversations, games, or activities; may start using other people's things without asking or receiving permission, adolescents or adults may intrude into or take over what others are doing).

(j) Tends to act without thinking, such as starting tasks without adequate preparation or avoiding reading or listening to instructions. May speak out without considering consequences or make important decisions on the spur of the moment, such as impulsively buying items, suddenly quitting a job, or breaking up with a friend.

(k) Is often impatient, as shown by feeling restless when waiting for others and wanting to move faster than others, wanting people to get to

the point, speeding while driving, and cutting into traffic to go faster than others.

(l) Is uncomfortable doing things slowly and systematically and often rushes through activities or tasks.

(m) Finds it difficult to resist temptations or opportunities, even if it means taking risks (A child may grab toys off a store shelf or play with dangerous objects; adults may commit to a relationship after only a brief acquaintance or take a job or enter into a business arrangement without doing due diligence).

B. Several noticeable inattentive or hyperactive-impulsive symptoms were present by age 12.

C. The symptoms are apparent in two or more settings (e.g., at home, school or work, with friends or relatives, or in other activities).

D. There must be clear evidence that the symptoms interfere with or reduce the quality of social, academic, or occupational functioning.

E. The symptoms do not occur exclusively during the course of schizophrenia or another psychotic disorder and are not better accounted *for by another mental disorder (e.g., mood disorder, anxiety disorder, dissociative disorder, or a personality disorder).*

Specify Based on Current Presentation

Combined Presentation: If both Criterion A1 (Inattention) and Criterion A2 (Hyperactivity-Impulsivity) are met for the past 6 months.

Predominately Inattentive Presentation: If Criterion A1 (Inattention) is met but Criterion A2 (Hyperactivity-Impulsivity) is not met and 3 or more symptoms from Criterion A2 have been present for the past 6 months.

Predominately Hyperactive/Impulsive Presentation: If Criterion A2 (Hyperactivity-Impulsivity) is met and Criterion A1 (Inattention) is not met for the past 6 months.

Inattentive Presentation (Restrictive): If Criterion A1 (Inattention) is met but no more than 2 symptoms from Criterion A2 (Hyperactivity-Impulsivity) have been present for the past 6 months.

It's that simple. Only six checks are needed. This is the newest version of DSM-V, published in 2013. Critics claim the newly added characteristics of ADD make diagnosis even easier for teachers and parents.

Thousands of studies about the disorder have produced differentiating results. Many question the disease because it's relatively new-a 1990's discovery. What did children pre-1990 do if they had problems concentrating? There were no pills to pop. They dropped out of school and/or found a trade or joined the military or raised a family-lived on, like everybody else. Sitting in a classroom was very difficult. The ADD/ADHD students of the old days were probably the class clowns or daydreamers who didn't perform well in academics.

Ritalin, manufactured by big-pharma Novartis, is the most common prescription for ADD/ADHD Disorder. Other brand name meds used are Adderall of Shire, Concerta of McNeil/Alza Corp., Dexedrine of GlaxoSmithKline, Focalin of Novartis, Metadate of UCB, Methylin of Mallinckrodt, Vyvanse of Shire, Daytrana of Noven

Therapeutics, and Quillivant of Pfizer. All of these pills are psycho-stimulants otherwise known as speed. Another option is the non-stimulant drug such as Strattera of Eli Lilly.

If these pills don't do the job, then antidepressants such as Elavil of AstraZeneca, Norpramim of Sanofi Aventis, Pamelor of Mallinckrodt, or Tofranil of AstraZeneca are given. Many parents are impressed with their children's performance after the drug starts affecting behavior.

So what happens once the ADD/ADHD child is medicated? Is the child easy to get along with? Does the child miraculously excel in school? Is the child medicated for life? Depends...

These drugs tend to work for about four hours in controlling the child's behavior. Some medications are in the process of making a pill that lasts for nine hours. Medication is usually taken before breakfast and skipped on the weekends and summer break.

A very general consensus among teachers and parents states the diagnosed ADD/ADHD children are compliant, calm, and much more focused. Many children have benefited off of the behavioral changes the drug promises.

Lindsey Tanner of the Associated Press wrote a 2009 article about a major study that took place in Chicago. Six hundred students with ADHD were followed from Kindergarten to fifth grade. This segment was divided into two groups, one group medicated and one group not medicated. The medicated children consistently scored three points higher on reading tests and five points higher on math tests, both standardized, than the children who were not medicated. Both the medicated and non-medicated students scored lower than the students without ADHD.

The biggest side effects are decreased appetite, weight loss, and insomnia. There have been few reports of paranoia, mania, hearing voices, and suicide (linked with anti-depressants).

Are ADD/ADHD meds too good to be true?
The study also shown that after three years of taking ADD medication the children were academically back to square one. Medication had

to be raised an average of 41% because of built up tolerance.

Some of the child's future career choices (pilot, law enforcement, and military) were disqualified for long use of the medication. Why? Because studies indicate that medications alter the brain permanently.

Is ADD/ADHD a fake disorder?

The Urban Dictionary defines ADD/ADHD (www.urbandictionary.com) as:

```
A fake disorder made up by doctors
and lazy parents, to give their kids
drugs and make them settle down.
"My kid isn't hyper. They have
ADD/ADHD."
It's also known as "fake-DD."
```

The Urban Dictionary is not alone. Many question the disorder's authenticity. Critics blast ADD/ADHD as a fake disorder invented by Big Pharma for the sole purpose of selling prescriptions that effectively control unruly behavior.

Dr. Leon Eisenburg, the inventor/father of ADHD, reportedly claimed the disease was a matter of fiction a few months before his 2009 death. Other doctors believe ADD and ADHD are not a disease or disorder, but a collection of symptoms of various health problems.

Neurologist Richard Saul believes that ADD/ADHD are phony diseases and need to be removed from the DSM-V. His book *ADD Does Not Exist* warns against the over-medication of drugs.

Most ADD/ADHD patients are treated with amphetamines. In 2006 stimulants received a black box warning from the FDA because of cardiovascular risks. Stimulants might improve behavior, but academic achievement is still an issue. Long-term effects of stimulants are still unknown, but there are links to substance abuse, height and weight stagnation during adolescence, and the potential for children to sell their prescriptions to peers as a recreational drug.

Lastly, medication for ADD/ADHD is big business. So-called experts in the ADD/ADHD field are paid for legitimizing this disorder which in turn sells more medication for treatment. For example, ADD Researcher Russell Barkley, Joseph Biederman of Harvard, and E. Fuller

Torrey have made small fortunes off of Big-Pharma in return for published studies and speaking and consulting fees that promote their products.

Whether ADD/ADHD deserves to be classed in the DSM-V remains a controversial subject. There is definitely something to the hyperactivity problems of some children. But how can a disorder that basically did not exist twenty-five years affect millions of children?

Chapter Nine

Why Are Medical Bills and Drugs So High?

Big Pharma did not get to the top of the economic heap by itself. The medical industry as a whole has been scratching each other's backs for decades. The partnership that has developed between Big Pharma and Big Medical has become the most successful merger in history. The way the two work together has driven up healthcare costs to an unprecedented level. Obamacare of 2014 will either prove to be a help or hindrance to the growing problem.

The complexity of interrelationships of the healthcare industry are daunting to the average layperson. The legal-ese and medical-ese are intentional, keeping us in the dark about how the game is played. The only thing we all can agree upon is the feeling of getting ripped off when examining a medical bill. Every hospital charges its patients differently. Price depends on insurance, lack of insurance, Medicare, and Medicaid.

Back in 2009 a student at the school I was working at dropped dead from a heart attack on the basketball court. This is somewhat common among teen athletes. The disease is officially called hypertrophic cardiomyopathy. Had the boy had a cardiac screening, this tragedy would not have happened.

My children played sports and I was worried. I called the health clinic which is now owned by a major hospital in my Chicago suburb. I volunteered to pay for the test myself if the insurance would not cover it. Several phone calls later, I still had not gotten an answer on how much the test cost. Two months went by and still no answer. I believe the hold-up had to be my insurance which was an excellent policy at the time. However, the test was not covered and my doctor wasn't sure what to charge. I never did get an answer. A few years later the screening was covered in the annual physicals and provided by most schools. I bring this up because that's how hospitals and clinics work-they either don't want to reveal their prices or don't know what their prices are once insurance is taken out of the equation.

The Chargemaster-What is it?

We've all heard of the "sticker price" of cars that no one supposedly pays. But even with shrewd negotiation, the customer still pays 90% or more of the price. The chargemaster is like the sticker price in a hospital or clinic. Unlike the auto industry, the range between the chargemaster's prices and the patient's bill is enormous. The pricing is not based on ability to pay, kind of like our tax system. Leaders within the medical world claim that chargemaster prices are for wealthy patients overseas. The inflated prices allow them to write-off their services for the poor. The only problem with this excuse is that the poor are also charged the chargemaster prices. Hospitals provide $39.3 billion in services for the poor that Congress picks up. The amount is based on chargemaster prices and not hospital costs. The real figure is closer to $3 billion.

Lawyers love chargemaster prices for civil suit cases because they jack up the bill. I could not find a common denominator on how the hospital boards come up with the prices.

How does Medicare fit in?

Medicare is an insurance program for U.S. citizens who are sixty-five years and older. Medicaid is part of Medicare and available for the poor. The program was signed into law in 1965 by President Johnson.

The program's biggest change occurred under President George W. Bush in 2003 when he signed the Medical Modernization Act which added prescription drugs as an additional benefit. In 2006, the donut hole took effect. The way it works makes the beneficiary have some out-of-pocket expenses.

-From 0-$295 Medicare pays nothing. This is what's considered the deductible of the plan.

-From $295-$2700 the patient pays 25% of the bill.

-From $2700-$6194 the patient pays 100% of the bill-the donut hole.

-Once the bill exceeds $6194, Medicare pays 95% of the bill. In 2010, Patient Protection

and Affordable Care Act enables the patient a
$250 rebate once in the donut hole.

Medicare typically picks up 80% of the patient's medical bills. Most Medicare patients have supplemental insurance to pay for the other 20% of the bill. Who pays for Medicare? The taxpayer. Healthcare costs are difficult to calculate. Some conservatively say costs were $300 million in 2013 while others claim Obamacare has so far cost $634 million (2013 and part of 2014). Medicare will pay for much of this bill. One of the good things that Medicare does is negotiate prices on certain tests, drugs, and services. Here are some common examples.

Troponin Test (measures proteins in blood) $199.50 standard price, $13.94 Medicare
Stress Test with radioactive dye/CT scan $7997.54 + $872 for dye standard price, $554 Medicare + $96 dye
$7.00 alcohol prep pad, $31.00 strap on table, $3.00 marker, $32 blanket warm-up, $39 surgical gown standard prices, Medicare 0.00 (part of the service)

According to many doctors and hospitals, the prices are too low, causing them to "lose" money.

Although Medicare can negotiate some prices, they can't negotiate prices on drugs despite being the pharmaceutical business's biggest customer. Their hands are tied by law or, more specifically, the taxpayers' hands are tied by law, protecting Big Pharma once again. The law states that Medicare has to pay 6% above the average drug price. Rebates given to doctors for prescribing certain drugs are not deducted from the "average" price.

Another disadvantage for Medicare/taxpayer is the inability to decide if a drug is a waste of money. It's called the comparative-effectiveness debate. For example, if Cancer Drug A costs a few hundred dollars and works as well as Cancer Drug B which costs thousands of dollars, Medicare cannot choose which one to pay for. The reality is that the doctor recommends the drug for his/her patient. Again, those within the healthcare industry cry that they can't make any money on Medicare/Medicaid patients.

Healthcare industry makes up 1/5 of the U.S. economy. To give an example of this enormity, let's start with Houston. Five of the city's top ten employers are hospitals. Surprised? New York City has eight out of eighteen top employers. To keep business booming, the healthcare industry keeps the money rolling by paying off Congress. Each member of Congress is lobbied by seven healthcare lobbyists. Since '98, 5.36 billion in campaign funds has been spent by the healthcare industry. By the way, that's more than Defense and Aerospace (1.53 billion) and oil and gas (1.3 billion) put together. If the healthcare industry is so broke, where are they getting billions of dollars to contribute to Congress? To compare the U.S. with other developed countries, the U.S. spends 27% more per capita. The brainwashing technique has many believing that we are "better." Are we 27% better?

Big Pharma keeps their customers rolling in by throwing their money at medical schools and physicians. In fact, the pharmaceutical industry is the single largest supporter and they get what they pay for-a school teaching to the tune of its donor.

U.S. healthcare cost has become an epidemic. Sixty percent of all bankruptcies have to do with medical bills. Almost half of working adults have problems paying off medical debt. The average American pays $8,000 per year in healthcare whereas Denmark pays $6,500 a year, Australia $5,000 per year, and Japan pays $4,000 a year. The U.S. doesn't have the highest life expectancy anymore. Japan does. The U.S is ranked fiftieth in the world for infant mortality.

People are taking busses to Canada or buying pharmaceuticals from Europe through the black market. Why? As already mentioned, those on Medicare might have prescriptions that put them in the pricey donut hole. Other people's insurance have caps on each year's claims and their health problems exceed the limits. And then there are others with no insurance and not poor enough to qualify for Medicaid.

So what do you do when you are sick and need certain kinds of medicine that is unaffordable?

You get creative. There is a black market of medicine and medical supplies. Canada, Mexico, and Europe are the suppliers.

Why does Big Pharma get away with charging more in the U.S. than other countries? This "magic" question has been swept under the rug for years. In 2013, the U.S. will spend $280 billion in prescriptions. Here are some examples of the mark-ups on drugs.

Lipitor costs 3 times more in the U.S. than Argentina.

Plavix costs 4 times more than in Spain.

Nexium costs 8 times more than in France.

I Rituximab INJ (cancer wonder drug): The average price paid by hospitals is $3,000-4,000. Hospitals charge the provider $13,702 at MD Anderson Center in Houston. That's pretty acceptable pricing. Rituxan is made by Biogen, a sister of Genetech. The company made $5.5 billion in sales for 2012. CEO George Scangos made $11,331,441 in 2011. Rituxan costs $300 to make, package, and ship per dose. So everyone gets rich-Genetech and MD Anderson Center. Everyone except the patient with cancer. To be fair, Genetech donated $2.85 billion in free medicine to the uninsured since 1985. That figure is based on what the product is sold for and not what it cost them. If adjusted, that would end up as less than 1% of their profits.

Another cancer drug that's a real cash cow is Flebogamma most commonly used in lymphoma. Flebogamma is a sterilized solution that boosts the immune system. Two companies sell it- Baxter and Grifols. The mark-up is unbelievable. The blood plasma is extracted from donors who are paid $25 each. After processing, packaging, and shipping, it costs Grifols somewhere between $200-300 dose. In Spain as in most European countries, Grifols can only charge a limited amount for "life-saving" drugs. Sloane-Kettering typically charges around $4,000 for a transfusion of Flebogamma. Medicare will only pay $2,123. After rebates, the hospital usually pays only $1400-1600 for a dose. Even with Medicaid's "rock-bottom" prices, that's quite a mark-up.

Hospitals provide $39.3 billion in services for the poor in which Congress pays for. This amount is based on chargemaster prices and not hospital costs. The real figure is closer to $3 billion. The 36.3 billion (remainder) is of course paid by the taxpayer.

Obviously, greed is the answer to U.S. drug prices being so expensive. But Big Pharma claims that Research and Development is the main reason why they charge such obnoxious prices. The reality is that only 15-20% of their gross revenue go into R&D. Grifols, the Flebogamma company, only spent 5%.

Do doctors over-test to be thorough or make more money?

The U.S. orders more CT scans/MRIs/x-rays than other developed countries. Why? You probably already know.

Medicare pays four times more CT scans than Germany. But Medicare is the only negotiator we have, right? Yes and no. There's a piece of legislation called the Services Access Protection Act that blocks Medicare from discouraging doctors from ordering too many CT scans. In 1997 there were 3000 scanners that each performed 3800 scans on average each year. In 2006 there were 10,000 scanners that each performed an average of 6100 scans per year. That's a quadrupling of CT scan usage. Who makes the CT scanners? Mainly G.E., a favorite corporation of Obama and Congress, and Siemans.

Why has the number of scans exploded?

Those in the healthcare industry cry lawsuits, but let's not forget how profitable it is to run these tests. Some experts believe that at least 60% of these tests are unnecessary.

Lab tests in all varieties are on the rise. One of the trends in healthcare is for big hospitals to buy out the middle man and take over all of the testing. 2013 estimates $70 billion alone in lab testing.

Nonprofit hospitals vs. For-profit hospitals: Is there a difference?

A nonprofit hospital is tax exempt. They are usually affiliated with charity and churches. Supposedly, they benefit the community with preventative healthcare education. They never turn away a patient based on inability to pay. Hospital staff on average is paid slightly higher than for-profit hospitals.

Forbes Magazine made a list of the most profitable hospitals in the USA.

http://www.forbes.com/2010/08/30/profitable-hospitals-hca-healthcare-business-mayo-clinic.html

Here are some of the highlights of 2010-2011.

Flowers Hospital-Dothan, Alabama (For-Profit 53% operating margin)

Del Sol Medical Center-El Paso, Tx (For-Profit 45% operating margin)

Rochester Methodist Hospital-Rochester, Minnesota (*NonProfit* 37% operating margin)

Saint Luke's Hospital-Cedar Rapids, Iowa (*Nonprofit* 36% operating margin)

Seton Medical Center Austin-Austin, Texas (*Nonprofit* 34% operating margin)

Swedish Medical Center-Englewood, Colorado (For-profit 33% operating margin)

Doctors Hospital of Augusta-Augusta, Ga (For-profit 33% operating margin)

Ohio State University Hospital-Columbus, Ohio (*Nonprofit* 32% operating margin)

Saint Mark's Hospital-Salt Lake City, Utah
(For-profit 31% operating margin)
Northridge Hospital Medical Center-
Northridge, California (***Nonprofit*** 30%
operating margin)
Lutheran Hospital of Indiana-Fort Wayne,
Indiana (For-profit 30% operating margin)
Erlanger Baroness-Chattanooga,
Tennessee (***Nonprofit*** 29% operating
margin)
Regional Medical Center Bayonet Point-
Hudson, Florida (For-profit 28% operating
margin)
Sutter Memorial Hospital-Sacramento,
California (***Nonprofit*** 28% operating
margin)
Eastern Idaho Regional Medical Center-
Idaho Falls, Idaho (For-profit 28% operating
margin)
Conroe Regional Medical Center-Conroe,
Texas (For-profit 28% operating margin)
Medical Center of Plano-Plano, Texas
(For-profit 28% operating margin)

St. Luke's Hospital-Jacksonville, Florida
(*Nonprofit* 27% operating margin)
Medical City Hospital-Dallas, Texas (For-profit 26% operating margin)
Memorial Medical Center-Las Cruces, N.M. (For-profit 26% operating margin)
St. Francis Medical Center-Monroe, Louisiana (**Nonprofit** 26% operating margin)
The Medical Center of Aurora-Aurora, Colorado (For-profit 26% operating margin)
Las Palmas Medical Center-El Paso, Texas (For-profit 25% operating margin)
Northwest Medical Center–Springdale, Arkansas (For-profit 25% operating margin)
St. Mary's Hospital-Rochester, Minnesota (*Nonprofit* 24% operating margin)

Out of the top twenty-five most profitable hospitals in the U.S., ten hospitals are nonprofit. So what does that mean? They don't pay taxes for income, sales, or property. Does that make them the biggest money makers of all? What do they do with their profits? There are no shareholders to make happy. They pay their top executives millions of dollars each year, expand the hospitals, buy the latest equipment, and continue increasing their costs. There is no law to prevent them from profiting. There are 2900 not-for-profit hospitals in the U.S. Here are the annual profits and CEO salaries:

1. Jeffrey Romoff, University of Pittsburgh Medical Center — $5.97 million
2. Delos Cosgrove, MD, Cleveland Clinic — $2.31 million
3. Herbert Pardes, MD, former CEO of NewYork-Presbyterian Hospital (New York City) — $4.35 million
4. Lars Houmann, Florida Hospital Orlando — $2.92 million
5. Thomas Priselac, Cedars-Sinai Medical Center (Los Angeles) — $2.77 million (2011)
6. Martha Marsh, former CEO of Stanford Hospital & Clinics (Palo Alto, Calif.) — $1.92 million
7. Steven Safyer, MD, Montefiore Medical Center (Bronx, N.Y.) — $4.07 million
8. Garry Scheib, executive director of Hospital of

the University of Pennsylvania (Philadelphia) —
$1.53 million

9. Sandra Gomberg, former interim CEO of
Temple University Hospital (Philadelphia) —
$508,753

10. John Hillenmeyer, former CEO of Orlando
Regional Medical Center — $2.24 million

11. Peter Slavin, MD, Massachusetts General
Hospital (Boston) — $2.5 million

12. Robert Garrett, Hackensack (N.J.) University
Medical Center — $1.83 million

13. Patrick Gavin, Crozer-Chester Medical Center
(Upland, Pa.) — $266,926 (named president in
July 2010)

14. Daniel Evans Jr., Indiana University Health
Methodist Hospital (Indianapolis) — $2.08 million

15. Elizabeth Nabel, MD, Brigham and Women's
Hospital (Boston) — $1.6 million

16. Larry Goldberg, former CEO of Vanderbilt
University Medical Center (Nashville, Tenn.) —
$842,854

17. Robert Grossman, MD, New York University
Langone Medical Center (New York City) — $3.49
million (includes compensation from related

organizations)

18. Ronald Hytoff, former CEO of Tampa (Fla.) General Hospital — $2.33 million

19. Kevin Wardell, president of Norton Hospital (Louisville, Ky.) — $743,592

20. Dean Harrison, Northwestern Memorial Hospital (Chicago) — $9.72 million

21. Thomas Lewis, former CEO of Thomas Jefferson University Hospital (Philadelphia) — $1.28 million (2011)

22. Susan Somerville, RN, executive director of North Shore University Hospital (Manhasset, N.Y.) — $839,734

23. Ron Girotto, former CEO of The Methodist Hospital (Houston) — $2.57 million (2009)

24. Ruthita Fike, Loma Linda (Calif.) University Medical Center — $997,707

25. Kevin Sowers, president of Duke University Hospital (Durham, N.C.) — $658,592

Other nonprofit CEO salaries: Red Cross $561,210, Alzheimer's Association 996,000, American Cancer Society 913,000, and Breast Cancer Research Foundation 753,000

Nonprofit hospitals are supposed to give back to the community. For example, if nonprofit hospital A got out of paying fifty million dollars in taxes, then in a perfect world it should have donated somewhere in that amount in services, charity, or something comparable.

In 2013 the city of Pittsburgh requested the tax exempt status of University of Pittsburgh Medical Center be yanked. They were audited and it appears that they provided half of the healthcare that they claimed on paper. They certainly aren't the first nonprofit to "exaggerate" their generosity.

Other hospitals report meager amounts of charitable care. For example, Cleveland Clinic donated 2.6% of its total revenues in 2010. Florida Hospital provided 5.5% of its revenues to charity. Orlando Health gave 3.5% in free charitable care. And by the way, the amount that is counted in healthcare services isn't the "real" amount, it's the good ol' chargemaster prices talked about earlier in this chapter.

Illinois attempted to revoke tax exempt status from three hospitals back in 2011, but Governor Pat Quinn came to their rescue, calling for specific requirements for charity care. Non-profits won the battle. They can continue to not pay taxes for an indefinite and undefined set of free services and charitable contributions.

Chapter Ten

Black Box Drugs

Many doctors are using the term Pharmageddon to describe some of the tragedies happening in the pharmaceutical world. The term refers to the medicine making the sick sicker. The death toll hits people in their 40s the most frequently, but all ages are affected.

Black Box drugs are available on the market, but have a warning on the label. The side effects can be disabling or even fatal. One example of a warning could be something somewhat harmless such as "safe for adult women who are not pregnant" or "used for adults and not for children". The warning could be much more serious, as in the case of SSRIs which have a "risk of suicide" warning on all of the labels. Sometimes an instruction sheet/guide will accompany the prescription. A doctor is supposed to have a conversation about the risks of the drug with his/her patient to whom he/she is prescribing it for. The pharmacist must also have a short conversation about the risks before handing the prescription over to the patient.

How does a drug get a black box warning?

During the drug's trials there are only a sliver of the population being tested. Once approved, the use is widespread and there is a more accurate way of seeing the user's reactions. Some believe the warnings are out of control. Over the last ten years there has been an explosion of drugs required to carry the black box warning on the label.

List of the more popular black box drugs

All SSRIs (anti-depressants) for children

Celebrex (non-steroidal anti-inflammatory drug) cardiovascular and gastrointestinal risks

Depo-Provera (contraceptive injection) loss of bone density

Avandia (diabetes) risk of heart failure or heart attack for patients with underlying heart disease

Antibiotics with fluoroquinolone such as Cipro, Levaquin, Avelox, Noroxin, and Floxin are linked with tendon ruptures and tendinitis

Chantix-depression and suicidal thoughts and/or actions

What happens when a prescription drug disables or kills?

The U.S. has had a "Just Say No" to drug policy for decades. Most people envision drug dealers peddling cocaine, heroin, ecstasy, crystal meth, and marijuana. Prescription drugs are cheaper, easier, and gaining momentum in teens and young peoples' recreational drug of choice. In some cases the pharmaceutical drugs are synthetic versions of the illegal ones. For example, hydrocodone is a prescription opiate identical to heroin. Big Pharma is the new drug cartel that is taking over America. Unlike Pablo Escobar and the Columbian cartels, Big Pharma does not have to worry about prison.

As mentioned previously, teens are at-risk with SSRIs when using them properly. However, many teens are using the SSRIs as a means to get high, making them even more dangerous. According to the White House Office of National Drug Control Policy, prescription drugs are second to marijuana used for recreational use. Seven of the top ten drugs to get high on are prescriptions. Many pharmaceutical drugs can become addictive. Almost 20% of Americans have used prescription drugs to get high.

Prescription drugs are the leading cause of death in America. About 450,000 preventable medication-related adverse events occur each year. These adverse events cause injuries or death in one out of every five hospital patients. In 2009, 4.6 million drug-related visits ended up in the emergency rooms of the U.S. More than half of these patients had adverse reactions to medications. Most of these patients were taking the medicine exactly prescribed.

Drugs that kill:

Vioxx, a painkiller from Merck, is probably the most infamous example of a prescription that not only backfired, but has caused death of 55,000 American users, most elderly. Some speculate it prematurely ended up to another half of million more lives. Merck was fined over five billion dollars, and *then* had their money-making drug recalled (2004). The drug was used to fight pain, especially in arthritis-related problems. The recall happened days before a medical journal was about to publish how Vioxx users were at risk for heart attacks and strokes. Merck allegedly had known about the potential risks before its 1999 release.

Merck spent one hundred million dollars a year on TV advertising for Vioxx. It soon became one of Merck's bestsellers, bringing in two billion dollars a year. Twenty-five million Americans were prescribed Vioxx. A class action suit dragged on, and then came almost five billion dollar settlement in 2007.

A little conservative math-8 years X $2 billion (a year in sales) – 800 million (in costs) = 15.2 billion and then subtract five billion in settlements and that's still 10.2 billion in revenue from one of their many pharmaceutical products. To be fair, fees and settlements were estimated closer to $7 billion. If this figure is more accurate, then they only made 8.2 billion in revenue.

What happened to the top mucky-mucks who made the important decisions to keep Vioxx on the market?

The CEO resigned and was replaced with one of the top executives with a 5yr/10million dollar contract. No one was charged with malfeasance. Merck is currently under fire for some of their other products including Fosamax, Januvia, Nuvaring, and Propecia.

Baxter, Bayer, and another Big-Pharma companies, recalled dozens of products in response to two hundred lawsuits. Most of them came from selling HIV and/or Hepatitis C blood infected to hemophiliacs. The companies allegedly knew they were using blood from high-risk donors and refused to take precautions. These companies continued to distribute their blood abroad after U.S. became aware of HIV and hepatitis transmission. Six thousand to ten thousand Americans became infected with AIDs plus thousands in Europe and South America.

Baxter, Bayer, and a few other companies were charged over one billion dollars in fines.

Pfizer had to dish out $2.3 billion for illegally promoting Bextra, Geodon, Zyvox, and Lyrica.

Bextra, a pain killer, accounted for $894 million in settlements. The drug's risk involved cardiovascular problems and Stevens-Johnson Syndrome, a deadly disorder that involves sloughing of the skin. Bextra was replaced with Celebrex, a drug supported by the FDA and also under fire. Celebrex, Bextra, and Merck's Vioxx are classed as COX-2 inhibitors, a category of drugs.

What happens when the fines are a small pittance in comparison to mammoth profits?

Nothing. There really isn't an incentive to change safety policy. It's much more profitable to write favorable results of your drug's trials, sell it with an enormous profit margin, and then use the American population as guinea pigs to see if it really does work as good as it is advertised.

How Corrupt is Big Pharma?

The answer varies from day to day, year to year, but here is a sampling of who we are dealing with.

Merck was allegedly caught by two of its scientists for faking vaccine efficacy data for mumps. The alleged fraud started with Merck devising a testing methodology that used a less virulent strain of the mumps virus in order to get their desired results. When that failed, they then spiked the blood samples with animal antibodies to make the vaccine look like it had a 95% efficacy rate. That also didn't work-two strikes and no vaccine. Merck then falsified the results so that they could make a deal worth hundreds of millions with the U.S. government for the vaccine.

But the story doesn't stop here. They submitted the phone results to both FDA and European Medicine Agency, and then attempted to buy the silence of its staff. Stephen Krahling, a virologist with Merck in 1999-2001, was threatened with jail if he reported fraud to FDA. Merck continued to conceal the reality about their mumps vaccine, even after mumps outbreaks in 2006 and 2009. Stephen Krahling and Joan Wlochowski, another virologist, filed a complaint (False Claims Act) in 2010.

The Obama administration has been criticized for lack of follow-up which causes many people to see this as confirmation of Merck's monopoly, fraud, and collusion. But there is still hope. In June of 2012, Chatham Primary Care filed suit against Merck. They claim that this stunt caused the target date of eradicating mumps of 2010 now pushed into 2020. Chatham represents all who were vaccinated with the bogus vaccine as far back as 1999.

GlaxoSmithKline (GSK for short) was fined three million dollars for bribing doctors, burying clinical trial information, and fraudulent marketing. This company reportedly paid Dr. Drew (Dr. Drew Show) $275,000 to promote Wellbutrin, an antidepressant.

The Wall Street Journal reported on July 3, 2012:

In June 1999, popular radio personality Dr. Drew Pinsky used the airwaves to extol the virtues of GlaxoSmithKline PLC's antidepressant Wellbutrin, telling listeners he prescribes it and other medications to depressed patients because it "may enhance or at least not suppress sexual *arousal" as much as other antidepressants do. But one thing listeners didn't know was that, two months before the program aired, Dr. Pinsky -- who gained fame as "Dr. Drew" during years co-hosting a popular radio sex-advice show "Loveline" -- received the second of two payments from Glaxo totaling $275,000 for "services for Wellbutrin."*

Pfizer was sued by pharmacy retailers for allegedly "overarching anticompetitive scheme" to keep generics off the market. These retailers accuse Pfizer of monopolizing the industry. Their cholesterol drug Lipitor was the main one in question. Pfizer makes $10 billion off of Lipitor each year. Can't blame Pfizer for not wanting to share. Like Merck, there have been no arrests.

Bribery: 2008-2011 at least fifteen pharmaceutical and medical device companies have paid $6.5 billion in fines in order to make accusations of fraud and kickbacks go away. Yes, it is illegal to pay doctors to prescribe your product. Prescriptions are supposed to be based on what is best for the patient. Big Pharma has circumvented this type of ethical dilemma by paying doctors to attend conferences and speak about certain drugs. In other words, if Big Pharma company A pays Dr. Doe 10,000 over the weekend to blather on about how great their pill is, is it more likely that Dr. Doe will prescribe the same pill to his patients in the future? I think we both know the answer.

Chapter 11

Vaccines: Prevention or Profit?

We have been brainwashed since birth into thinking that vaccinations will save us from horrible diseases and influenza. The government forces our children to be vaccinated before entering public school, claiming that group safety is priority in keeping contagious germs at bay. Like sheep, we trust that this is all in our best interest and then, without giving it a second thought, take our children to the doctor multiple times for multiple shots before they reach kindergarten. Is this a good thing?

Celebrities such as Jenny McCartney, Brittany Spears, and Charlie Sheen have spoken out against vaccinations. They are not alone. Vaccines have been victim to conspiracy theories for decades. Like many other parents, I question their effectiveness and safety.

I am a mother with two healthy children who have been vaccinated with all mandatory and recommended shots for public school. My research has made me second guess these decisions. Other vaccinations, especially the flu vaccination, have never been taken. Again, I am not a doctor, but the lack of these shots has never made anyone in my household unduly sick with the flu. On the other hand, people in my family and at my work believe flu shots are a necessary part of flu season. Vaccinations of all kinds need a second look.

The very definition of a vaccine is

Injection of a killed microbe in order to stimulate the immune system against the microbe, thereby preventing disease. Vaccinations, or immunizations, work by stimulating the immune system, the natural disease-fighting system of the body. The healthy immune system is able to recognize invading bacteria and viruses and produce substances (antibodies) to destroy or disable them. Immunizations prepare the immune system to ward off a disease. To immunize against viral diseases, the virus used in the vaccine has been weakened or killed. To only immunize against bacterial diseases, it is generally possible to use a small portion of the dead bacteria to stimulate the formation of antibodies against the whole bacteria. In addition to the initial immunization process, it has been found that the effectiveness of immunizations can be improved by periodic repeat injections or "boosters.

In short, a vaccine is a disease alive or dead that is injected inside of us. To spare you the science lesson, it has proven to work in several cases, especially polio, but it doesn't work for every disease.

Vaccines have been around since 1000 CE. China figured out that one can fight disease with the actual disease by changing one's immunity. However, the credit for the first official vaccination goes to Dr. Edward Jenner of England. He figured out that cow pus injections protected one against smallpox in 1796. His methodology caught on around the world. Louis Pasteur came up with the rabies vaccine. His Germ Theory of Disease paved the way for the invention of other vaccines like polio.

Other ground-breaking vaccines such as Mumps, Measles, and Rubella (MMR) came along and the rest is history. Measles, Mumps, Polio, Dyptheria, and Rubella are eliminated in the West. By 2010, only seven countries were not immunized against polio. And that's not because the vaccines weren't offered from the U.S. and other countries. Parts of the Muslim world were suspicious of the materials used in the vaccine. Many believed the West was trying to sterilize them.

Eventually, vaccines attracted the attention of governmental regulation. Schools made immunization mandatory for enrollment. The mandates caused the vaccine business to skyrocket. More vaccines were invented and more mandates required people to get immunized.

In the 1950s there were thirteen required doses of diphtheria, tetanus, pertussis, and small pox given to children beginning at age two. By the 1980s the number went up to seven vaccines with a total of fifteen doses. By 2010 children were recommended to have sixty-nine doses of sixteen vaccines by age eighteen. The U.S. recommends the more vaccines than any other country.

How does a vaccine get "recommended" for use in the U.S.?

The Advisory Committee on Immunization Practices or ACIP is responsible for telling us what vaccinations we need. The ACIP consists of fifteen voting members who are selected by the Department of Health and Human Services. Like the FDA and USDA and WTO and so many other organizations, there are ties to vaccine manufacturers/Big Pharma. The ACIP holds three meetings each year at the Center for Disease Control and Prevention (CDC) to talk about outbreaks and new vaccines up for recommendation.

The CDC works like a public relations spokesman for vaccine manufacturers. They enthusiastically promote the vaccines by offering incentives to states for the number of vaccines issued. One example involved the Ohio Department of Health. A million dollar bonus was handed out because of successful campaign that vaccinated a target number of children.

There are other important groups that contribute to vaccine mandates such as the American Academy of Pediatrics (AAP). This group along with the CDC determine the number of shots that are given for a baby well-visit. The AAP took $100,000 from Merck for their new building headquartered in the Chicago suburbs.

Can Big Pharma recommend or even mandate their products?

That's not how it's supposed to work, but yes. As mentioned before, mandates equal gigantic profits. With a patent and guaranteed customer base, a company can't help but be hugely successful. Here are some examples.

Merck, a Big Pharma company, has many creative ways to get their vaccine publicized. Merck created/bankrolled the Illinois Health Coalition which works as a dummy organization to endorse their products. Merck's vaccines got a boost in sales with the help of Senator Grace Drake, Republican from Ohio Senate. She was an integral part in legislating SB 224, a mandate for the Hepatitis B vaccine for Ohio kindergartners. The senator once presided over the Health and Human Services Committee and received generous campaign contributions from Merck.

Dr. Paul Offit of Philadelphia, one of Merck's consultants, gave a conference that supported making chicken pox vaccinations mandatory. Merck was working on the chicken pox vaccine at the time and stood to gain seven million dollars for each new class of kindergartners in Ohio alone. On a side note, chicken pox vaccine is made from the lungs of two aborted fetuses.

Dr. Paul Offit has the nickname Dr. Paul "for profit" Offit. The $350,000 grant he took from Merck was just the beginning to their lucrative relationship. Offit invented Merck's Rotateq vaccine which is used for the rotavirus in infants. When Offit was on the ACIP board, he voted 'yes' three times on the panel in relation to his vaccine. The ACIP had one stipulation in regards to conflict of interest. Offit couldn't vote for a universal recommendation for all babies to receive the Rotateq. No worries. His ACIP colleagues pulled his weight and voted "yes" for him. His vaccine was conveniently added to the CDC's childhood vaccine schedule.

In 2008 Rotateq sold for $182 million. Profit was huge and unreported. Merck was said to receive somewhere between $29-55 million. Dr. Offit once said, "an infant can safely receive up to 10,000 vaccinations at once and 100,000 in a lifetime." Dr. Offit received $1.5 million for research plus a multi-million dollar salary as a chair for Children's Hospital which is funded by Merck.

Are flu shots a scam?

Although not yet a mandate, flu shots are recommended to everyone starting at six months old.

The 2009 Swine Flu scare was one of the mildest influenza seasons to date. Australia banned the vaccine for children under five years old because of links to Guillan Barre Syndrome, a killer nerve disease.

Swine flu might not have been the pandemic the media reported, but the flu's profits proved contagious. In 2009 conservative estimates put swine flu earnings in the billions with another $10 billion pledged for more swine flu research.

Tamiflu is another vaccine that's quite the money maker. It was the response to the avian flu pandemic that was responsible for an estimated 1-2 million deaths. George W. Bush purchased (with taxpayers' money) twenty million doses at $100/dose-$2 billion. Tamiflu turned out to be worthless. At best, it might have reduced the time one was sick with the H5N1 virus, but could have caused additional problems.

Bush stockpiled fifty million doses of Tamiflu. The doses were purchased from Roche. Roche had licensed a company called Gilead Sciences who invented the Tamiflu. From 1997-2001 Donald Rumsfeld was the chair of Gilead.

Did Rumsfeld have a stake in the company? If so, how much?

In 2005 Rumsfeld, the Secretary of Defense under Bush, was the largest stockholder in Gilead, earning 10% from every dose of Tamiflu sold. Reminder-Good ol'Donald Rumsfeld was also the head of Searle when aspartame was almost rejected from FDA approval. He certainly has a gift of being at the right place at the right time-a real Midas touch.

Does the flu shot work?

The shots claim to have a 60% effective rate, but other reports say there is a 1.5% of the population who take the vaccine. The problem with flu viruses is that scientists have to predict the top three viruses that will be the most prevalent for the year.

Ingredients found in the flu shot copied from: https://usahitman.com/frwngafs/

- *2-Phenoxyethanol is an anti-bacterial agent being used as a replacement for the preservative Thimerosal (mercury). It's considered a very toxic material that could cause a boatload of side effects, including behavioral disorders ... vomiting ... diarrhea ... visual disturbances ... convulsions ... rapid heart rate ... central nervous system disorders ... depression ... kidney, liver and blood disorders ... and reproductive defects.*

- *Aluminum shows up in vaccines in many forms – like aluminum phosphate, aluminum hydroxy phosphate sulfate and aluminum hydroxide, to name a few. It works as an "adjuvant" to stimulate your immune system's response to the virus in the vaccine. The problem is ... aluminum is a particularly dangerous neurotoxin. It has the ability to slip past your body's natural defenses and enter your brain – potentially causing brain damage ... Alzheimer's disease ... dementia ... convulsions ... and coma. Human and animal studies have shown that aluminum can even cause nerve death.*

- ***Ammonium Sulfate*** *is a substance commonly added to pesticides. It's not known at this time if it's cancer-causing, but it has been suspected of gastrointestinal, liver, nervous system and respiratory system toxicity.*
- ***Beta-Propiolactone*** *ranks high as a hazardous chemical on at least five federal regulatory lists. It caused lymphomas and hepatomas after being injected into lab mice, but its true effect on humans is not known. Due to animal study results, the International Agency for Research on Cancer (IARC) has classified beta-propiolactone as a possible human carcinogen.*
- ***Formaldehyde*** *is used as a preservative to stabilize the vaccine. It's a colorless, flammable, strong-smelling chemical that's mostly used in industry to manufacture building materials and produce many household products. Plus, it's also used to embalm – and preserve – dead bodies. (Remember the frog in your high school biology lab?) Formaldehyde is suspected of weakening the immune system and causing neurological system damage ... genetic damage ... metabolic acidosis (excessive blood acidity) ... circulatory shock ... respiratory insufficiency ... and acute renal (kidney) failure. It's been classified as a known human carcinogen (cancer-causing*

181

substance) by IARC and is ranked as one of the most hazardous compounds on at least eight federal regulatory lists.

- **Formalin** *helps preserve the vaccine. It's a mixture of formaldehyde, methanol and water. It's mostly used to preserve tissue samples in health care laboratories and presents the same danger to your health as formaldehyde does.*

- **Gentamicin Sulfate** *is an antibiotic that's been known to cause deafness or loss of equilibrioception (sense of balance). It can also be highly nephrotoxic (damage your kidneys) if multiple doses accumulate over time.*

- **Monosodium Glutamate (MSG)** *excites and poisons your cells and tissues. It's used as a stabilizer in vaccines and is also found in many processed foods. MSG has been shown to cause retinal degeneration ... behavior disorders ... learning disabilities ... reproductive disorders ... obesity ... and even lesions on the brains of lab animals. Allergic reactions to MSG can be severe.*

- **MRC-5 Cellular Protein** *is human diploid cells taken from aborted human fetuses. They're used as a culture to grow the virus.*

- **Neomycin** *is an antibiotic that has been shown to have multiple effects on your body. It can be a* *neurotoxin and an ototoxin (affect hearing and balance). It also can cause respiratory paralysis, kidney damage and kidney failure. Plus, it retards your vitamin B6 absorption, sometimes leading to mental retardation and epilepsy. Some allergic reactions to neomycin can be life threatening.*

- **Octoxinol-9** *is a vaginal spermicide.*
- **Phenol** *is included in vaccines to help stimulate immune response. Instead, it does the opposite – by inhibiting phagocytic activity. Phagocytes are your body's first line of defense. They engulf and digest antigens and activate the other elements of your immune system. Phenol's phagocytic-inhibiting effect actually hinders your immune system from properly dealing with the pathogens that are entering your body through the vaccine.*
- **Phenol** *is used in the production of drugs, weed killers and synthetic resins, so you can imagine the effect it has on the human body. It's considered to be toxic to your cardiovascular, gastrointestinal, nervous, reproductive and respiratory systems ... your liver ... your kidneys ... and your skin. Phenol is so deadly that is was used by the Nazis as a means of extermination during the World War II. Phenol injections were given to thousands of people in concentration*

183

camps – especially at Auschwitz-Birkenau – to kill those who were mentally ill, had incurable tuberculosis and were permanently incapable of work.

- ▪ ***Polymyxin B*** *is an antibiotic with some nasty side effects – neurotoxicity and acute renal tubular necrosis (the most common cause of kidney failure).*

- ▪ ***Polysorbate 80 (Tween-80)*** *works as a stabilizer in the vaccine. It's used in a wide variety of products including ice cream, milk products, vitamin tablets, lotions and creams and medical products like vaccines and anti-cancer medications. But it's not as safe as it sounds. According to the December 2005 issue of Annals of Allergy, Asthma and Immunology, polysorbate 80 can affect your immune system and cause severe anaphylactic shock, which can kill. It also causes cancer in animals.*

- ▪ ***Streptomycin*** *is an antibiotic. Its main side effect is ototoxicity – the loss of hearing.*

- ▪ ***Thimerosal*** *is used as a preservative in the vaccine. It contains 49.6% mercury by weight and has been implicated in many health conditions, such as cardiovascular disease ... autism ... seizures ... mental retardation ... hyperactivity ... dyslexia ... and many more* *nervous system conditions. The mercury used in vaccines is second in toxicity only to the radioactive substance, Uranium. It's a powerful neurotoxin that can damage the entire nervous system of an infant in no time.*

- *Plus,* **the inclusion of aluminum and even formaldehyde with the mercury in the vaccine magnifies** *the problem. Aluminum can make the mercury 100 times more toxic. Toss in formaldehyde as well, and one independent study found that mercury toxicity was increased by 1,000 times.*

Dr. Hedwig Kresse, a vaccine analyst, predicted in 2007 that vaccine profits will reach or exceed $16 billion in 2016. Wyeth's (a Big Pharma company) Prevnor vaccine is one of the many reasons for this prediction. The vaccine is given to infants as a vaccine against pneumonia and meningitis.

In 2000 Prevnor cost $320 for four doses. It was added to mandatory vaccinations during baby well-visits. Add a few more mandates currently being considered like a pertussis vaccine in California for children in 7th-12th grades and New York's mandatory flu shots for health care workers only strengthen Dr. Kresse's prediction. There are one hundred and forty-five vaccines in the pipelines, waiting for the market.

With the explosion of vaccine inventions along with the government's leverage in their promotion and enforcement, there is money to be made. That's where Big Pharma comes in. Two to four vaccines a year enter the medical world promising everything from cancer prevention to protection from auto-immune diseases. Sounds too good to be true. Who wouldn't want that kind of protection? Everyone lives longer, healthier lives while Big Pharma makes even more money. What's to complain about?

Mumps, Measles, and Rubella (MMR) and Hepatitis B are two of the vaccines that anti-vaxxers, (basically a naysayers of all vaccines) like to jump on. The major problem is the thiomersal ingredient. This is a mercury based compound used as a preservative. It's highly toxic. Studies show a connection with Multiple Sclerosis, especially with the Hepatitis B vaccine.

There are several other links to other diseases, especially autism. The thiomersal is also the ingredient many find to be suspicious. Today one in sixty-eight children are diagnosed with autism, a 30% increase from 2012. The mass increase has yet to be explained.

Regardless to growing health concerns, vaccines are a major cash cow. And who says Americans don't manufacture anything anymore? Lehman Brothers (the company left out of TARPs bailout) predicted vaccines would grow an annual rate of 18%. They were wrong. Vaccines are growing at a 24% rate. Vaccines are classed as a blockbuster drug or a drug that sells more than one billion dollars a year. It was vaccines that caused two giants to merge. Pfizer bought Wyeth ($68 billion in cash) because of their vaccines.

Sanofi of France is currently the biggest supplier of flu vaccines. They had $1.2 billion in vaccine sales for 2012 and expect to increase sales by 50% with more contracts. GlaxoSmithKline raised the price of their Fluarix by 50% as well. Vaccines will reach $3.7 billion this year in global sales. There are more ways to receive immunizations. Nose spray is becoming a more preferred way to ingest the vaccines, but it's more expensive.

What can a parent do about vaccinations?

There are exceptions for vaccination mandates. Religious reasons exempts children from vaccinations in all states except for Mississippi and Virginia. There are personal and philosophical exemptions in eighteen states.

Conclusion

I began this book knowing very little about Big Pharma and Big Agri. After a great deal of research, New World Order connections emanated off of the computer screen. Politics has always been the most obvious link to globalization. One world government has been reflected in international policies, wars, and alliances for centuries. But a world government cannot be achieved through government alone.

The genetically modified food industry has expanded across the globe. Monsanto has been controlling the U.S. food policy for decades. With the Codex and World Trade Organization backing it up, Europe has set the perfect foundation for the world to control food and supplements. Through the FDA and patent law, both Big Pharma and Big Agri are given all of the help needed to create monopolies all over the world. Is this an intentional takeover? *Another book...*

In the U.S. pharmaceuticals bankrupt the sick and their families all in the name of capitalism. If there wasn't enough disease to profit off of, more diseases and disorders continue to be

189

invented or exaggerated or even caused for an even bigger bottom line. Meanwhile, harmful, if not blatantly fatal, mistakes are often made and the price is a drop in the ocean when compared to annual earnings. The U.S. is the most expensive healthcare system in the world, a fact that fascinates me since most hospitals set arbitrary prices hidden inside of the chargemaster. Could any other business in the U.S. multiple sets of prices for the same services without customers screaming 'discrimination'?

Where does Obamacare fit into all of this? It's too soon to tell. A few of my sources who work in mid-level/high-level healthcare management believe that Obamacare is really a takeover of healthcare. That's one-fifth of the U.S. economy. Separately, I was told that this program is financially unsustainable. We've all heard about the royally screwed-up website. Incompetence was to blame. But there's so much more to it. Apparently, one hand does not know what the other hand is doing. If one signs up for Obama-care, he/she can then print out their coverage health card and then, without paying, go get the expensive operation that they have been putting off. My sources believe that it could be years before the IRS or whoever will be running the bills will catch up with those who do not pay for the policies. Again, is this incompetence or is this an intentional dissolution of the U.S.? *Another book….*

This research has made me pay much more attention to food while adding herbs and vitamins to my diet. My cabinet is now stocked with turmeric, glucosamine, Vitamin D3, and many other health supplements. I continue to question unnecessary tests and the prices that are charged. Again, I am not a doctor, but I feel empowered to question doctors on their decisions instead of just going along with whatever they say.

Whether you believe in New World Order or not, whether you believe in Big Pharma's and Big Agri's role in New World Order or not, I hope this book opened your eyes to the food that you eat and the health care that you receive. I hope you question the mainstream media and their lack of news stories on Big Agri and Big Pharma. The mainstream media is another engine that drives New World Order. *Again, another book…*

I would love to hear your thoughts and views on this subject. Please drop me an email, tweet, Facebook post, or blog comment. If you feel this book educated you in some way, please rate it on Amazon. Your feedback is very important to me.

blcsdina@gmail.com

www.dinaraeswritestuff.blogspot.com

@haloofthedamned

FB:

https://www.facebook.com/DinaRaeBooks?ref_typ e=bookmark

Website: http://dinarae.co/

My bibliography is very informal. Some of my sources are directly hyperlinked to the text. For readers with the paperback version of this book, email me if curious about a source. Other sources listed below are less direct, but nonetheless pertinent to my research. Some online articles did not include the author.

Bibliography

Sources Indirectly Used
Throughout the Book

Crane, Ian
http://www.ianrcrane.co.uk/index.php?act=viewPro
d&productId=12
Codex Alimentarius Lecture by Ian R. Crane,
http://www.youtube.com/watch?v=O2D4-noTiCg
CODEX ALIMENTARIUS,
http://foodcode.blogspot.com/2007/11/new-world-
order-codex-alimentarius.html
Ian R. Crane: Surviving The Final Meltdown...
Financial Terroris...
http://www.youtube.com/watch?v=8mcXsInxlHY
Interview with Ian Crane via phone

Engdahl, William "Iraq and Washington's 'seeds
of democracy"

http://www.engdahl.oilgeopolitics.net/GMO/Iraq_a
nd_seeds_of_democracy/iraq_and_seeds_of_dem
ocracy.HTM

Horn, Tim "The Food and Drug Administration:
The Process of Approval"

http://www.thebody.com/content/art14537.html

Jones, Alex, www.infowars.com

Big Pharma Giving Little Girls Cancer: Alex Jones Report
https://www.youtube.com/watch?v=9lQqMQj7iX8

Syrett, Richard Radio Show: The Conspiracy

Show

http://www.theconspiracyshow.com/

Turbeville, Brandon TYRANNICAL "HEALTH STANDARDS" OF THE NEW WORLD ORDER
http://www.infowars.com/tyrannical-health-standards-of-the-new-world-order/

Natural News, www.naturalnews.com
Adams, Mike "Big Pharma criminality no longer a conspiracy theory: Bribery, fraud, price fixing now a matter of public record"
http://www.naturalnews.com/036417_Glaxo_Merck_fraud.html#ixzz35i0wEj9E
http://www.naturalnews.com/gallery/documents/Merck-False-Claims-Act.p...
"New FDA leadership has strong ties to Big Pharma, Wall Street"
http://www.naturalnews.com/020029_Byron_Richard_Andrew_von_Eschenbach.html#ixzz35i1PLvOD

FDA employee admits Aspartame is Poison. The New World O...
https://www.youtube.com/watch?v=Yj5E68FxT-4

(This one is kind of funny)

PHARMACEUTICAL MONOPOLY, Interview with Dr Rath PART 1,
http://www.youtube.com/watch?v=KFPR0x9 3CIY

How the FDA Changed Over Time
http://www.youtube.com/watch?v=2PcY9UNsmVI

The Sad Truth about the FDA Approval History

http://beforeitsnews.com/conspiracy-theories/2012/12/the-sad-truth-about-the-fda-approval-history-2447066.html

SSRI Stories, Antidepressant Nightmares

http://ssristories.com/index.php

EVERY THIRTY MINUTES FARMER SUICIDES, HUMAN RIGHTS, AND THE

AGRARIAN CRISIS IN INDIA by NYU School of Law

http://www.chrgj.org/publications/docs/every30min .pdf

Sources Used in Specific Chapters

Chapter Two: FDA and USDA: Puppets or Protectors?

EconTalk.org host: Russ Roberts (Stamford)
Guest Marcia Angell of Harvard was Ed. In Chief
of NE Jrl of Med. 11/19/2012 Radio Show

"Pharmaceutical Patent Lengths"
http://progressiveproselytizing.blogspot.com/2011/
04/pharmaceutical-patent-lengths.html Apr 14,
2011

Maughan, Jaceson "How Long Does a Drug
Patent Last"
http://www.life123.com/career-money/business-
law/patents/how-long-does-a-drug-patent-
last.shtml

Chapter Three: What is a GMO?

Null, Gary (post) "Seeds of Death"

http://www.youtube.com/watch?v=eUd9rRSLY4A&fea
ture=share

Jameson, Marni "Nonprofit Hospitals: Do They
Give Back Enough?"

http://articles.orlandosentinel.com/2013-04-
27/news/os-nonprofit-hospitals-community-
benefits-20130426_1_orlando-health-avertano-
furtado-taxes

Chapter Seven: The Rise of Anti-Depressants

Bornfeld, Steve "Antidepressants most popular prescription medication in U.S."
http://www.lvrj.com/health/antidepressants-most-popular-prescription-medication-in-u-s-128168918.html

Kresser, Chris "The dark side of antidepressants"
http://chriskresser.com/the-dark-side-of-antidepressants

Veracity, Dani "Antidepressants Linked to Suicide and Violence"
http://foodmatters.tv/articles-1/anti-depressants-linked-to-suicide-and-violence

Wayne, Michael "Antidepressants: Widely Used, But Practically Useless?"
http://www.lowdensitylifestyle.com/antidepressants-widely-used-but-practically-useless/

"A Short History of SSRIs"
http://www.blizzardlaw.com/antidepresssant-lawsuits/history-of-ssris

"Mass Violence Caused by Anti-Depressants and SSRI Drugs"

http://medicalwhistleblower.blogspot.com/2011/09/
mass-violence-caused-by-anti.html

Chapter Eight: ADD/ADHD: Is it a Real Disorder?

Baughman, Fred "Does ADHD Exist?"
http://www.pbs.org/wgbh/pages/frontline/shows/m
edicating/experts/exist.html

Stellpflug, Craig "ADHD: Misdiagnosed and
Overmedicated"
http://www.naturalnews.com/036056_ADHD_over
medication_children.html

Tanner, Lindsey "ADHD Drugs Linked to Better
Test Scores"
http://usatoday30.usatoday.com/news/education/2
009-04-27-adhd-tests_N.htm

"When the Diagnosis is ADHD"
http://consults.blogs.nytimes.com/2011/02/15/whe
n-the-diagnosis-is-a-d-h-d/

Diagnostic Criteria for Attention
Deficit/Hyperactivity Disorder
http://www.addforums.com/forums/showthread.ph
p?t=100858

What is Hyperactivity?
http://kidshealth.org/kid/health_problems/learning_
problem/adhdkid.html

Chapter 10-Black Box Drugs

Mercola, Dr. "Prescription Drugs Now Kill More
People than Illegal Drugs" 7/3/13
http://healthimpactnews.com/2011/prescription-
drugs-now-kill-more-people-than-illegal-drugs/

The 6 Top Thugs of the Medical World... As
Ranked by "Top 100 Corporate Criminals" List

http://articles.mercola.com/sites/articles/archive/20
10/11/18/drug-companies-are-ranked-in-the-top-
100-corporate-criminals-of-the-1990s.aspx

Fictional Works by Dina Rae

Novels (Available by Major Distributors)

Halo of the Damned

Halo of the Nephilim

Bad Juju

The Last Degree

Short Stories

Halo of the Madonna

Be Paranoid Be Prepared

www.ingramcontent.com/pod-product-compliance
Lightning Source LLC
Chambersburg PA
CBHW060253290526
45789CB00001B/317